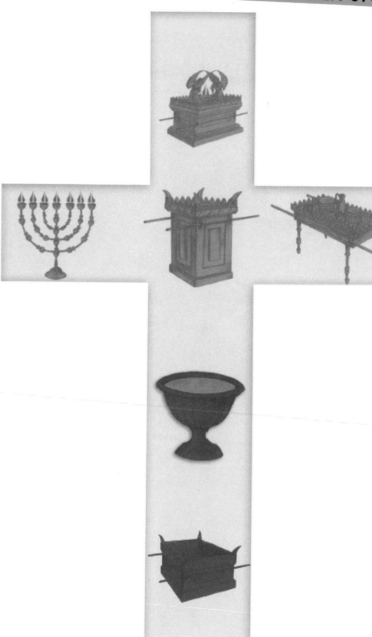

SEEING CHRIST *in* *the* TABERNACLE

Ervin N. Hershberger

Vision Publishers
Harrisonburg, VA

First	edition	1995
Second	printing	1996
Third	printing	1999
Fourth	printing	2002
Fifth	printing	2002
Sixth	printing	2003
Seventh	printing	2004
Second	edition	2007

Published by Vision Publishers
Harrisonburg, Virginia

ISBN: 1-932676-18-X

For additional copies or comments write to:
Vision Publishers
P.O. Box 190
Harrisonburg, VA 22803
or
Call 877-488-0901
Fax 540-432-6530
Email orders@vision-publishers.com
www.vision-publishers.com
(see order form in back)

Table of Contents

Credits Due

God the Father, God the Son, and God the Holy Spirit, without whom we can do nothing of eternal value, and without whose blessing the whole project would still be a failure!

Calvary Bible School Board and personnel for suggesting and requesting that this book should be written.

Calvary Publication Board for their encouragement.

Richard Polzyn, Millersburg, Ohio, for editing my manuscript.

Marvin E. Yoder for studying the manuscript and giving valuable suggestions.

Lynford Dale Yoder (age 15) for most of the art work.

Lyndon Eugene Yoder for drawing the Court and the specified location of the tribes.

Simon Schrock, Fairfax, Virginia, for his voluntary letter of encouragement, which I incorporated as a Foreword.

Others who have read the manuscript, offered encouragement, and all who gave their prayer support.

Especially my wife Barbara for her assistance, support, sacrifices, encouragement, and patience with me at times when I neglected other duties while engrossed in study and writing.

May our precious Saviour and Lord be praised, honored, and glorified! That is what the Tabernacle is all about.

Foreword

by Simon Schrock

Jesus Christ is my only hope for a blessed eternity and my very purpose for living. Therefore I make a special effort to read books about Him. I do this to focus my mind on Christ and to know Him more intimately. What a serendipity I found in *Seeing Christ in the Tabernacle*. It was like an oasis!

Here I was reading about the Tabernacle from the Old Testament books of Exodus and Leviticus (which are supposed to be somewhat dry reading). But soon it was like a curtain being pulled open, and I began to see Jesus Christ, the Son of God. Most of the pages in this little volume focus on Jesus Christ.

Among the books about Jesus, this one stands out so significantly that I plan to return to its pages for future studies. If you are looking for something that will deepen your understanding of Jesus and your love for Him, you can find a rich experience by studying the Tabernacle with this author.

It is useful for personal or group study. If you do not have a high appreciation for the Old Testament Scriptures because they do not seem to be relevant for today, I encourage you to read this book. It has been a blessing to me!

I recommend that you avail yourself of *Seeing Christ in the Tabernacle*. It's like finding a refreshing drink in an unexpected place.

Preface

The treasures of Christ are far too numerous, too deep, and too marvelous for us to comprehend them all at a glance. Surface truths are open and obvious, yet many of them escape our notice for many years. Treasures of hidden gems lie waiting beneath the surface to reward the search of all who desire to learn what God yearns to reveal to us of Himself and of Christ.

God was grieved when Eve ignored His command and listened to the serpent. To the serpent He said, "I will put enmity between thee and the woman, and between thy seed and her SEED; it [her SEED] shall bruise thy head, and thou shalt bruise HIS heel" (Gen. 3:15). Behind those capitalized words lay hidden TREASURES of truth which God chose to reveal little by little. He knew the SEED would die—and would rise again the *third* day!

By design God had chosen the *third day* of Creation to bring dry land up out of that watery mass, to bring forth grass, herbs, and trees (Gen. 1:9-13). That typifies resurrection! I think God delights to have us look for those hidden treasures of truth.

In the tenth generation of mankind God selected a man to build an ARK (Gen. 5:3-29). The Ark was a *type* of Christ, while Noah and his family were a *type* of the Church, safe in Christ. God steered that Ark to be just at the right place to rest "in the *seventh month on the seventeenth day of the month,* upon the mountains of Ararat" (Gen. 8:4). As the flood waters receded, the Ark was lifted out of the water on the *seventeenth day* of the month *Abib.* Nearly 2400 years later Jesus rose from the dead on that very day! I don't think that *happened* by coincidence.

8

In the twentieth generation (Gen. 11:10-29) God revealed through Abraham that an "only son" (Gen. 22:2, 12, 16) was to be offered. Although Abraham did not actually slay Isaac, the Bible says he "offered up his only begotten son" (Heb. 11:17). In his heart Abraham had already offered Isaac before he "clave the wood for the burnt offering" (Gen. 22:3). On the *third day* (vv.4, 11-13) he received him even from the dead, in a figure (Heb. 11:19). These are God-given types and shadows all pointing directly to Jesus Christ, and their precision is utterly amazing!

Six generations after Abraham, God called Moses to lead His people out of Egypt, and to write the Pentateuch. God Himself provided all the details He wanted written about the twenty-five generations that preceded Moses. Christ is definitely the central theme from Genesis One through the Revelation. We have cited only a few of the highlights pointing to Jesus Christ.

Moses, God's chosen founder of Old Testament law, was an official foreshadow of Christ, God's chosen Founder, Prophet, and Judge of New Testament order (Dt. 18:15, 18). Mosaic sacrifices were only "a *shadow* of good things to come, and not the very image of the things" (Heb. 10:1). "*The body is of Christ*" (Col. 2:17). Types and shadows are God's picture gallery, primarily foreshadowing the Person and work of Jesus Christ throughout. Those gems of truth are worth digging for!

In addition to types specifically so named in the Bible, there are many other fascinating projections in the Old Testament depicting the Person and ministry of Christ in the New Testament.

Before the Tabernacle was built, God instituted the Passover. But first of all He reconstructed the Hebrew calendar, giving the last half of the civil year significant preeminence over the first half. Of the seventh month, Abib, God said, "This month shall be unto you the beginning of months: it shall be the first month of the year to you" (Ex. 12:2).

We can well understand why Abib, the Passover month, was to have the preeminence. In the month Abib God delivered Israel out of Egypt (Ex. 13:3; 23:15; 34:18; Dt. 16:1), preplanned as a foreshadow of a much greater deliverance: "For even Christ our passover is sacrificed for us" (1 Cor. 5:7).

The name Abib was changed to Nisan (Neh. 2:1; Esther 3:7) during the Babylonian Captivity, but that did not change the month nor the day. God had selected the fourteenth day to be the Passover, and that was the very day Jesus died on Calvary.

We have noticed several early foreshadows of a *third-day* resurrection. Types do not verify truth, they only illustrate what the Bible verifies. Jesus Himself declared repeatedly that He would *"rise on the third day"* (Mt. 16:21; 17:23; 20:19; 27:63-64; Mk. 9:31; 10:34; Luke 9:22; 18:33; 24:7, 46). We believe He Knew, and we accept His word as Truth. 1 Corinthians 15:4 confirms it again.

If the right people had known that the fifteenth day of Nisan was always "an holy convocation" (Lev. 23:5-7), "an high day" (John 19:31), a *sabbath* surpassing the weekly sabbath, we might observe *Good Thursday* instead of Friday. There are only two nights between Friday evening and Sunday morning, and Jesus plainly said He would "be three days and three nights in the heart of the earth" (Mt. 12:40).

Hebrew days began in the evening, extending from sundown to sundown. Jesus and His disciples ate their Passover supper in the evening, most likely after sundown of the thirteenth day, which was the beginning of the four-teenth day of Nisan.

At Jesus' trial the next morning, the Jews "went not into the judgment hall, lest they should be defiled; but that they might eat the passover" (John 18:28). That afternoon, shortly after the ninth hour (Mark 15:34-38) Jesus died on the cross, the very event portrayed by every Passover since Exodus 12.

We have ample reason to believe that Jesus did rise on the third day, just as He had repeatedly predicted. And I do believe that the third day was the seventeenth day of Abib/Nisan, as foreshadowed by the Ark on Mount Ararat in Noah's day.

The Purpose of this Book

This book is a study of God's masterpiece of typology, the Mosaic Tabernacle. The Tabernacle is a fascinating object lesson, a picturesque illustration of Christ and His Church on earth. Unless we see some aspect of Jesus Christ in every piece of its furniture, boards, pillars, ropes, and curtains, we have not sufficiently studied the Tabernacle.

Our primary purpose, however, is not the Tabernacle, but to adore, praise, and glorify Jesus Christ, of whom the Tabernacle is only a shadow. Our second purpose is to encourage diligent Bible study. This book was written at the request of Calvary Bible School personnel, and with Bible schools in mind. I believe there is ample material for a three-week Bible school course, even with one hour class periods. Those with forty-five minute classes will need to be selective about what to cover.

Each chapter concludes with QUESTIONS FOR DISCUSSION to help facilitate your study. We do not provide formal answer keys as such, but the majority of answers are found in the text. Others, not found in the text, are clearly stated in the Bible. For example: answers to number 17 in Chapter Eight and number 6 in Chapter Twelve are not found in this book, but they are found in 1 Corinthians 11:3-7 and Exodus 32:26 respectively. A few questions are designed not so much to require specific answers, but to stimulate serious thinking.

We believe the book would be equally suitable for Sunday evening or midweek Bible study groups, for the family worship hour, or for private personal study. It is not intended to be an independent *study book* apart from the Bible, but is designed to assist you in your STUDY OF THE BIBLE.

"Incline thine ear unto wisdom, and apply thine heart to understanding; . . . if thou seekest her as silver, and searchest for her as for hid treasures; then shalt thou understand the fear of the Lord, and find the knowledge of God" (Prov. 2:2-5).

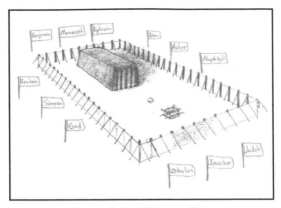

The Tabernacle and Courtyard showing
where each tribe camped.

Introducing the Tabernacle

AN OBJECT LESSON WORTHY OF INTENSE STUDY

The story of the Tabernacle reaches deeper than the earth, higher than the sky, and farther than the universe. Its humble features represent none of these, but they represent the Creator of them all, our Lord and Saviour, Jesus Christ. Every piece, feature, and service of the Tabernacle teaches us something about Christ and His Church here on earth.

God called Moses to Himself in the thick cloud upon Mount Sinai (Ex. 24:12). During those forty days God showed him an exact pattern of the Tabernacle they were to build, giving precise dimensions and specific details. It is evident that every detail was important to God. Repeatedly He emphasized making all things according to the pattern He showed to Moses in the mount. Heb. 8:5; Ex. 25:9, 40; 26:30; 27:8; Nu. 8:4; Acts 7:44).

God used two relatively short chapters (Gen. 1 and 2) to record the creation of the universe. But He used fifty chapters (13 in Exodus; 18 in Leviticus; 13 in Numbers; 2 in Deuteronomy; 4 in Hebrews) to explain the construction of the Tabernacle, its features, furniture, and the services to be held there. Obviously the Tabernacle was very important to God.

GOD'S PREVISION MADE PROVISION

Before God brought Israel out of Egypt, He provided, through the Egyptians, an abundance of material for building the Tabernacle. Read Exodus 3:21-22 and 12:35-36. It worked! God's way always works. Why did God tell the Israelites to "borrow" from the Egyptians something they would never return?

Remember that God is the Owner of everything. Even "we are not our own" (1 Cor. 6:19). We are only stewards of what God entrusts to our care. The same was true of the Egyptians, who had enslaved the children of Israel, evidently without pay. Therefore it was absolutely right for God to collect from the Egyptians material He had entrusted to their care. It was all His, and it was right for Him to give it to Israel as *back pay* for their many years of hard labor in Egypt.

With that material God taught Israel the Biblical principle of giving *willingly* (Ex. 25:1-9; 35:5-9, 21, 22, 29), a primary principle for Christian giving. This principle was demonstrated by the Macedonian churches (2 Cor. 8:1-5) in that they "first gave their own selves to the Lord" (v. 5). Then "the abundance of their joy and their deep poverty abounded unto the riches of their liberality. For to their power, . . . and beyond their power they were willing of themselves" (8:2, 3). The children of Israel, experiencing the same joy, willingly brought "much more than enough for the service of the work" (Ex. 36:5). They had to be restrained from bringing more (verse 6).

GOD SELECTED THE BUILDING FOREMEN

God specified where each tribe was to camp, and where in the procession each tribe should march as they traveled. The tribe of Judah was to go *first* (Nu. 2:9), and the tribe of Dan "shall go *hindmost*" (2:31). It was by design that God chose Bezaleel from the tribe that went *first*, to be the chief foreman. Then He chose Aholiab from the tribe that came *last*, to be his teammate (Ex. 31:2-6; 35:30-35). Conjointly, they typified Christ, who is both the FIRST and the LAST (Isa. 44:6). He is "Alpha and Omega, the beginning and the end, the FIRST and the LAST" (Rev. 1:8, 11, 17, 18; 2:8; 22:13). He is "the *author* and *finisher* of our faith" (Heb. 12:2, emphasis mine).

Moreover, Judah (*praise*—Gen.29:35) was the kingly line, of whom Jacob said, "thy father's children shall bow down before thee" (49:8). This prefigured Christ as our coming King (49:10), yea, the "KING OF KINGS AND LORD OF LORDS" (Rev. 19:16). For God has said, "I will overturn, overturn, overturn . . . [other kings], until he come whose right it is; and I will give it him" (Ezek. 21:27).

Dan (*God hath judged*—Gen. 30:6), marching last, may remind us that our final Judge is Christ. "For the Father judgeth no man, but hath committed all judgment unto the Son: that all men should honour the Son, even as they honour the Father" (John 5:22, 23a). "A bruised reed shall he not break, and smoking flax shall he not quench, till he send forth *judgment unto victory*" (Mt. 12:20).

The Tabernacle, being portable and temporary, typified Christ and His Church on earth. Bezaleel (meaning *under God's shadow*) and Aholiab (meaning *tent* of the father), were appropriately named to be the building foremen of the Tabernacle. They beautifully picture Christ building His Church on earth (Mt. 16:18).

Solomon's temple, being a stationary building of nonperishable material, typified Christ and His Church in heaven.

In any study of typology, always keep in mind that we do NOT use types to establish doctrine, but to illustrate and teach doctrine that is already established by the Scriptures.

TYPOLOGICAL KEYS TO MEMORIZE AND REMEMBER

(To remember the keys helps to understand the Tabernacle)

The type of some of these is identified by the Bible. For most of them the conclusion is simply drawn from the way they are used. Admittedly some of them may be debatable. To me the collective evidence is impressive, but if found in error, I gladly welcome corrective instruction. The most important goal of this study is that Christ be lifted up and glorified.

A. Symbolism Attached to Materials and Colors

1. Gold — (as used herein) The deity and glory of Jesus Christ
2. Silver — Atonement (Ex. 30:13-16)
3. Brass — Judgment (Lev. 26:19; Nu. 21:8-9; Dt. 28:23)
4. Blue — The Heavenly One (The atmospheric heavens are blue.)
5. Purple — The Royal One (Known as the royal color.)
6. Scarlet — The Suffering Servant (Atoning Blood)
7. Fine Linen — The righteousness of saints (Rev. 19:8)
8. Goats Hair — Primarily the Fatal Sin of Man (Rom. 5:12) Plus The Sin Offering (Isa. 53:10; 2 Cor. 5:21)
9. Rams' Skins dyed red — Consecration—obedient unto death
10. Badgers' Skins — Unlimited protection in Christ
11. Shittim Wood — Incorruptible Humanity of Christ (Ps. 16:10b)
12. Oil — Typifies the Holy Spirit (Spirit of Christ)
13. Sweet Spices — Jesus' beautiful, fragrant life (Ex. 30:34-38)
14. The Veil — "That is to say, his flesh" (Heb. 10:20)

B. Symbolism Attached to Numbers and Measurements

One	Unity
Two	Fellowship; Union with Christ; Two are a Witness
Three	The Trinity, or Triune Godhead
Four	Earth (Four winds; four corners of the earth)
Five	Grace (Quite evident in typology studies)
Six	Man; Human weakness (Short of perfection-Rom. 3:23)
Seven	Perfection (Seven or seventh 549 times in the Bible)
Eight	New Beginning (New world began with 8 people; new week)
Nine*	Spirit Fruit (Gal. 5); Nine Beatitudes; self repeating*

Ten	Responsibility on earth; Completeness
Eleven	Human failure; Confusion; Judgment
Twelve	Number for earthly government (12 tribes; 12 Apostles)
Forty	Testing; Probation (Jonah 3:4; Luke 4:2)
Fifty	Year of Jubilee (Lev. 25:8-17)

In measurements involving half-cubits, each half-cubit becomes a *unit* of measure. For example:

$1^{1}/_{2}$ cubits = *three* half-cubits (Three—Trinity)
$2^{1}/_{2}$ cubits = *five* half-cubits (Five—Grace)

Moreover, baking, beating, bruising, burning, crushing, piercing and roasting may well remind us of Christ's suffering. For example: *beaten* gold (Ex. 39:3), *roasted* lamb (Ex. 12:9).

Memorizing the typological keys given in the Introduction is quite important for speedy comprehension of this study.

Books on Tabernacle study usually have the student start in the outer court and work his way in to the Holy of Holies. Using those books I taught it that way for several years. Then I was convicted of the fact that salvation and holiness are GOD'S work. It never began with man, nor in the outer court! It began with Christ in the highest Heaven—the Holy of Holies.

In His building instructions to Moses, God began with the Ark (Ex. 25:10), which represents Christ Incarnate: i.e. on earth, in a body of flesh. Salvation and holiness both begin and end with Christ in God. Therefore our study of the Tabernacle begins with the Ark, where God began with His instructions to Moses.

(*Note: If 9 is multiplied by any number and the digits in the product are added together, the sum is nine: 3x9=27 (2+7)=9, 9x9=81 (8+1=9), 789x9=7101 (7+1+0+1=9). In some cases, the addition process must be carried further to accomplish this: 11x9=99 (9+9=18 [1+8=9]), 546x9=4914 (4+9+1+4=18 [1+8=9]), 951x9=8559 (8+5+5+9=27 [2+7=9]). There are no exceptions.

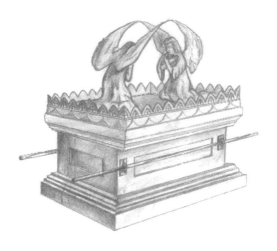

CHAPTER ONE

I. THE ARK OF THE COVENANT, A MOST HOLY VESSEL

Exodus 25:10-16; 37:1-5

The Ark was made of shittim wood overlaid with gold inside and outside. Shittim wood (sometimes called iron wood) is of the acacia family, of which there are many varieties. The shittim tree, said to reach a maximum height of about twenty-five feet, does produce some valuable timber. It is a hard wood, resistant enough to heat and decay that it has been described as indestructible. Such durability appropriately typifies the incorruptible body of Jesus, *prepared* for His incarnation (Heb. 10:5). As it is written, "neither wilt thou suffer thine Holy One to see corruption" (Ps. 16:10b; Acts 2:27; 13:35).

The Ark, completely overlaid with gold within and without, reminds us that Jesus retained full deity in union with His humanity. Throughout the Tabernacle, wood typifies His humanity and gold His deity. Though He had voluntarily emptied Himself of some of the unique attributes and prerogatives of Deity (Phil. 2:6-8), "to be made like unto his brethren" (Heb. 2:17), He was nonetheless God, even in the flesh.

To be our Daysman (Job 9:33) Christ needed to be equally

representative of God and man. No one but Jesus ever qualified to thus bring God and man together. He was not a hybrid
(half God and half man), but He was fully God and fully
Man. In fact, had He been less than God, His sacrifice would
not have sufficed for the atonement; and had He not been
fully Man, the atonement would not have applied to man.
"For verily he took not on him the nature of angels [conse-
quently atonement does not apply to angels]; but he took on
him the seed of Abraham" (Heb. 2:16), "to make reconciliation for the sins of the people" (v.17c).

The Ark especially emphasizes the PERSON of Jesus, while
the Mercy Seat emphasizes His PURPOSE. The efficacy and
validity of the atonement rest equally upon His *Godhood* and
His *Manhood*. Both are absolutely essential as a BASE for
the Mercy Seat (Propitiation #2435*; Rom. 3:25). The
crown of gold upon the Ark (Ex. 25:11) foreshadows "the *man*
Christ Jesus" (1 Tim. 2:5), promoted and exalted as "KING
OF KINGS, AND LORD OF LORDS" (Rev. 19:16).

Dimensions (Ex. 25:10) and Typological Suggestions

Length: $2\frac{1}{2}$ cubits = 5 half-cubits or units of measure: 5 = Grace.
Breadth and height: $1\frac{1}{2}$ cubits = 3 half-cubits: 3 = Trinity
Vertical girth: $4 \times 1\frac{1}{2}$ = 6 cubits: 6 = the number of man.
Horizontal girth: $2 \times 2\frac{1}{2} + 2 \times 1\frac{1}{2}$ = 5+3 = 8 cubits: 8 = New Beginning

Maybe that's manipulating numbers, but it simply illustrates what the Bible plainly teaches: the Trinity (3), by
Grace (5), offers Man (6) a New Beginning (8). "If any man
be in Christ, he is a NEW CREATURE: old things are passed
away; behold, all things are become NEW" (2 Cor. 5:17).
WHAT A BONUS!

"And. . . the Levites bare the ark of God upon their shoulders with the staves thereon, as Moses commanded
according to the word of the Lord" (1 Chron. 15:15). This
reflects the high respect and reverence with which the Ark
was to be borne.

*Index number in Strong's Concordance.

THE CONTENTS AND THEIR SYMBOLISM

1. The Tablets of Stone (called the Testimony—Ex. 25:16) with the Ten Commandments engraved in stone, represent God's law. "Yea, thy law is within my heart" (Ps. 40:8b). Like those stones were *kept* in the Ark, so God's Law was fully KEPT (i.e. *observed* and *preserved*) by Christ.

All of us have broken God's Law. Only in Christ (typified by the Ark) can we be pardoned, cleansed, and safely covered by the Blood-sprinkled Mercy Seat.

2. The Golden Pot of Manna (Ex. 16:32, 33) typifies Christ as the Bread of Life, eight times declared to be the true Bread that came down from heaven (John 6:32-35, 48-58).

3. Aaron's Rod that budded (Nu. 17:10) depicts Resurrection: *Life out of death.* Christ our Mediator verily rose from the dead! "In him was life" (John 1:4). He could truly say, "I am the resurrection, and the life: he that believeth in me, though he were dead, yet shall he live: and whosoever liveth, and believeth in me shall never die" (John 11:25, 26). "Because I live, ye shall live also" (John 14:19b).

I. VIOLATING THE HOLINESS OF THE ARK WAS PUNISHABLE BY DEATH (DENYING THE DEITY OF CHRIST MAY BE ETERNALLY FATAL!)

Safety was not in the Ark of the Lord but in the Lord of the Ark. Some 530 years later, Israel had forsaken the Lord of the Temple and trusted in "the temple of the Lord" (Jer.7:4). Tragedy followed both errors.

Today, unfortunately, some people rely on Communion (the Table of the Lord), while slighting the Lord of the Table.

A. Tragic experience taking the Ark into battle (1 Samuel 4)
  1. Slaughter in the army, 4:10

2. Sons of Eli, 4:4, 11
3. Eli himself, 4:12-18
4. Phinehas's wife, 4:19-22

B. Tragedies Encountered by the Philistines (1 Samuel 5)
   1. At Ashdod, 5:6
   2. At Gath, 5:8-9
   3. At Ekron, 5:10-11

C. Tragedy Struck Israel at Bethshemesh (1 Samuel 6)
   1. The Ark was returned after seven months, 6:1-18.
   2. 50,070 Israelites died because some of them had looked into the Ark, 6:19-21.
   3. To look into the Ark they had to lift the Mercy Seat, exposing themselves to the Law that they had broken. Exposure to the broken Law without benefit of the Mercy Seat would mean death to any of us! See 1 Samuel 6:19, NASB.
   4. Uzzah touched the Ark and died immediately for his error (2 Sam. 6:6, 7; 1 Chron. 13:9-14). Later the move was completed safely, using the prescribed methods, 15:25-29.

Do we need any more proof that true holiness is inviolable?

II. TWO OTHER ARKS ALSO TYPIFIED CHRIST

A. NOAH'S ARK was a beautiful type of Christ. The universal death sentence (Gen. 6:7) could not be reversed, but God's grace provided a way to rise above it. Not one soul perished in the Ark. It mattered not how heavy the torrent, how furious the tempest, nor how deep the tide; the Ark rose triumphantly above it all. Like Christ, it provided absolute safety for all who abode within, but it could help no one on the outside.

B. The Ark of Bulrushes (Ex. 2:3) was neither big nor strong, but it was safely sealed. As long as baby Moses stayed in, and the mighty waters stayed out, all was well.

That little Ark triumphantly carried baby Moses upon the very waters in which he had been sentenced to die (Ex. 1:22), and Moses became a son in the house of him who had pronounced the sentence! Likewise, by believing and abiding in Christ, we can become sons and daughters of Him who said, "The soul that sinneth, it shall die" (Ezek. 18:4). That sentence remains unchanged, "But thanks be to God, which giveth us the victory through our Lord Jesus Christ" (1 Cor. 15:57). Christ is our Ark of safety!

QUESTIONS FOR DISCUSSION

1. Why did Christ need to become Man to bring us salvation?
2. How did incarnation affect His relationship with the Father?
3. When and how did Jesus become God's *begotten* Son?
4. Did the Old Testament ever call Him Son except prophetically?
5. What did it cost Him to condescend from Infinity to infancy?
6. What did it cost Him to pay the price of our redemption?
7. What shall He have as His reward? Philippians 2:9-11.
8. What lessons should we learn from the life of Jesus?
9. What does the incorruptibility of shittim wood portray?
10. What does abiding in Christ imply and require?
11. What are the practical evidences of Christ working *in* us?
12. What are the manifestations of Christ working *through* us?
13. Why did they KEEP the Tablets of Stone in the Ark?
14. What's the only possible way for us to KEEP the commandments?
15. What does the budding of Aaron's rod portray about Jesus?
16. How did the Manna represent Christ as the True Bread?
17. How does Noah's Ark typify Jesus?
18. How is our experience in Christ similar to Noah in the Ark?

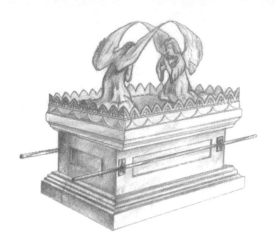

CHAPTER TWO

THE MERCY SEAT, CHERUBIM, AND SHEKINAH GLORY

I. THE MERCY SEAT

Exodus 25:17-22; 37:6-9

The Ark emphasized the PERSON and the Mercy Seat emphasized the PURPOSE of Christ. The Mercy Seat was a plate of pure gold: no wood. Nothing but Deity could offer saving mercy. In all the universe there was no moral, sinless blood to be found, except that of the sinless Lamb of God. All human blood is immoral because of sin. Animal blood is non-moral; therefore "it is not possible that the blood of bulls and of goats should take away sins" (Heb. 10:4). The sin debt had to be paid with Heaven's currency.

The Mercy Seat is where God met with Moses (Ex. 25:22). For Moses "heard the voice of one speaking unto him from off the mercy seat that was upon the ark" (Nu. 7:89). The Mercy Seat typifies Christ, where "mercy and truth are met together; righteousness and peace have kissed each other" (Ps. 85:10). Peace and reconciliation are obtainable only through Christ, typified by the Blood-sprinkled Mercy Seat. Ephesians 2:13-19.

Christ, our Mercy Seat, is a place of rest for the sin-sick soul. Jesus calls entreatingly, "Come unto me, all ye that labor and are heavy laden, and I will give you rest. Take my yoke upon you, and learn of me; for I am meek and lowly in heart: and ye shall find rest for your souls" (Mt. 11:28, 29).

In Christ, God rests His lawful case against us, "wherein he hath made us accepted in the beloved" (Eph. 1:6).

"When I see the blood, I will pass over you" (Ex. 12:13). "For it is the blood that maketh an atonement for the soul" (Lev. 17:11).

THE LENGTH AND BREADTH of the Mercy Seat are identical with the Ark: 1½ cubits wide = 3 half-cubits: 3 suggests Trinity; 2½ cubits long = 5 half-cubits: 5 the number of Grace, essential to Mercy; 3 + 5 = 8 the number of a New Beginning.

The length plus breadth (2½ + 1½) = 4: number of earth. There will even be a new earth when Jesus comes (Isa. 65:17; 66:22; Rev. 21:1)! Christ the God-Man (typified by this gold/wood combination) fits and fills precisely every requirement of divine holiness, justice, judgment, grace, and mercy. Keep in mind that we do not use types to establish doctrine, but to illustrate doctrine already established by the Scriptures.

The thickness of the Mercy Seat is nowhere stated. Unnamed dimensions suggest boundlessness, something that is infinite. That is certainly true of God's grace and mercy. We sing, "There's a wideness in God's mercy," and how true that is!

Remember, however, that the Mercy Seat is exactly the same width and length as the Ark, not one inch more.God's eternal mercy is wide enough and long enough to cover everyone who ABIDES in Christ. But there is a day coming when His wrath will be poured out without mixture [no mercy] upon all those who do not abide in Christ (Rev. 14:10).

In Chapter One we noticed the golden crown upon the Ark (Ex. 25:11), which proclaims the Man Christ Jesus as "KING OF KINGS, AND LORD OF LORDS" (Rev. 19:16). His deity and His humanity are inseparable. This

Mercy Seat fits down right inside that golden crown, and is held securely in place by the crown.

Christ's rightful position is forever secure, regardless of unbelieving men or demonic forces. He is "the propitiation for our sins" (1 John 2:2; 4:10); there is no other (Acts 4:12; 1 Tim. 2:5; Phil. 2:9-11).

II. THE CHERUBIM

Exodus 25:18-20; 37:7-9

Angels are "ministering spirits" (Heb. 1:14), basically noncorporeal, but able to take on visible form when needed for the benefit of man. Cherubim are considered guardians of God's holiness. (*Cherubim* needs no "s" to make it plural.)

Over the Mercy Seat were two cherubim. "Beaten out of one piece . . . out of the mercy seat made he the cherubim" (Ex. 37:7, 8). This may be giving recognition to Christ as their Creator in the beginning (John 1:3; Col. 1:16). "He that sanctifieth and they who are sanctified are all of one" (Heb. 2:11).

The cherubim were not fashioned of molten gold poured into a mold, but beaten out of the two ends of the Mercy Seat. God had filled His workmen with His Spirit so that they could make everything the way He directed them (Ex. 31:2-6; 35:30-35). Otherwise it would seem to be impossible to shape the cherubim and the lamp stand by beating.

Beating denotes suffering. If angels rejoice when a sinner repents (Luke 15:7, 10), they probably suffer grief when a soul goes astray. They may have agonized intensely while Jesus was dying on the cross, but they were restrained from intervening.

Reverently and fervently they guard the inviolable holiness of God. Their steady focus on the Shekinah Glory reflects the angels' interest in God's marvelous plans, "which things the angels desire to look into" (1 Peter 1:10-12). It is God's intention that the holy angels ("the principalities and powers in heavenly places") might now by the Church learn to know "the manifold wisdom of God, according to the eternal purpose which he purposed [and fulfilled] in Christ Jesus our Lord" (Eph. 3:10, 11).

III. THE SHEKINAH GLORY, or
"THE GLORY OF THE LORD"

The word Shekinah is not found in the Bible. It is the name given to the manifestation of God's presence, by which He appeared "in the cloud upon the mercy seat" (Lev. 16:2c). It was a flame of glory, enclosed in a cloud for man's protection.

Ever since the fall of man, God often manifested His presence by fire: "a flaming sword which turned every way" at the east of the Garden of Eden (Gen. 3:24); "a flame of fire" at the burning bush (Ex. 3:2); "like a devouring fire" on Mount Sinai (Ex. 24:16, 17); "for our God is a consuming fire" (Heb. 12:29; Dt. 4:24).

At least ten times the Shekinah Glory appeared outside the Holy of Holies: five times in warning of judgment when the people murmured (Ex. 16:7-10; Nu. 14:1-10; 16:19, 42; 20:6), and five times in blessing when they did well (Ex. 24:16, 17; 40:34, 35; Lev. 9:23; 2 Chron. 5:14; 7:1).

Finally, six and a half years after Ezekiel had been carried captive to Babylon, the Lord brought him "in the visions of God to Jerusalem" (Ezek. 8:1-4). There he saw the Glory of the Lord departing from apostate Israel in four reluctant steps: (1) It left the Mercy Seat and stood over the threshold of the house (Ezek.10:4). (2) It rose from off the threshold (10:18,19) and apparently hovered over the midst of the city (11:23). (3) It "went up from the midst of the city, and stood upon the mountain [Mount of Olives] which is on the east side of the city" (11:23). (4) While it lingered there, the Spirit of God took Ezekiel back to Chaldea, and the vision went up from him (11:24).

No more do we read of the glory of the Lord in Israel, except prophetically (Ezek. 43:2-5; 44:4; Hab. 2:14), until Jesus was born in Bethlehem. Then an angel appeared to the shepherds, announced the birth of Christ, "and the glory of the Lord shone round about them" (Luke 2:9). For thirty-three years the glory of the Lord indwelt Jesus here on earth (John 1:14).

Once, upon the Mount of Transfiguration, it shone

through, "and his raiment was white as the light" (Mt. 17:2); "exceeding white as snow; so as no fuller on earth can white them" (Mark 9:3); "white and glistering" (Luke 9:29).

Forty days after Jesus had risen from the dead, He led His disciples out to the Mount of Olives one more time. "And it came to pass, while he blessed them, he was parted from them, and carried up into heaven" (Luke 24:51). This was the same Mount from which Ezekiel had seen the glory of the Lord taken up into heaven some six hundred years earlier.

Ten days after Christ's ascension, near the end of a ten-day prayer meeting in an upper room, the Glory of the Lord reappeared in the form of "cloven tongues like as of fire, and it sat upon each of them" (Acts 2:3). Today it indwells His church, awaiting the Rapture, to ascend once more to heaven from whence it came.

QUESTIONS FOR DISCUSSION

1. The Mercy Seat was PURE GOLD—no alloy. What's the message?
2. Define propitiation (Rom. 3:25; 1 John 2:2; 4:10).
3. By whom and how is propitiation accomplished?
4. What was ABSOLUTELY UNIQUE about the blood of Christ?
5. How does it differ from animal blood and from human blood?
6. Define the Old Testament function of the Mercy Seat?
7. What is the Living Mercy Seat doing today?
8. Why was the Crown not on the Mercy Seat?
9. Where were the cherubim and what was their function?
10. What do angels desire to look into (1 Pet. 1:12), and why?
11. Where was the Shekinah Glory? What did it signify?
12. On what ten occasions did the Glory openly appear?
13. When and how did Ezekiel see the Glory depart from Jerusalem?
14. Why did the Glory depart? Where did it go? Ezek. 8:3—11:24
15. When, where and how did it return, and in whom did it abide?
16. With whom did the Glory depart the second time?
17. When did it return, and in whom does it abide today?

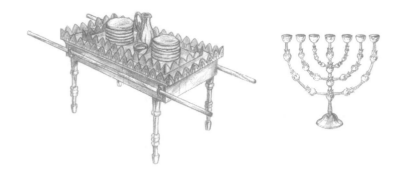

CHAPTER THREE

THE TABLE, SHEWBREAD, LAMPSTAND, AND OIL

I. THE TABLE FOR THE SHEWBREAD
Exodus 25:23-29; 37:10-16

The Table, made of wood, represented Christ in the flesh. Completely overlaid with pure gold, it reminds us of His continuing deity as well. He became fully Man to be made Living Bread for us, but He retained His deity that He might be our Eternal Life. "For ye are dead, and your life is hid with Christ in God. When Christ, who is our life, shall appear, then shall ye also appear with him in glory"(Col. 3:3).

The Table was one cubit wide (unity), two cubits long (fellowship, union with Christ), one and one-half cubits high (suggestive of the Trinity). Tables naturally remind us of fellowship, especially the Lord's table (1 Cor. 10:21). True fellowship, however, depends on unity, and all fellowship with Christ inevitably involves the Trinity. As the priests had fellowship together with their high priest at this table, so also do Christians have fellowship together with their High Priest,

Jesus Christ, at the New Testament communion table. All the way around the Shewbread Table was a border. The German says it was a handbreadth *high* (Ex. 25:25). Someone interpreted the border as representing Bible helps such as commentaries, concordances, etc.[1] I beg to disagree. Notice that it was topped with a golden crown, certainly unbecoming for manmade books. There are four crowns in the Tabernacle, jealously (Ex. 20:5) reserved for the Lord Jesus Christ. He alone is "KING OF KINGS, AND LORD OF LORDS" (Rev. 19:16)!

The Hebrew word translated border is defined by Strong as "something *enclosing*; a *stronghold*" (# 4526). Since it is the only measurement in the Tabernacle given in handbreadth instead of cubits, and since it *encloses* twelve loaves representing the twelve tribes, it certainly reminds us of the Lord's protecting Hand around His people. The crown is the symbol of His authority and power to protect and to keep His own. See Isaiah 49:15, 16.

II. SHEWBREAD, MEANING PRESENCE BREAD

EXODUS 25:30

"And thou shalt take fine flour, and bake twelve cakes thereof: . . . And thou shalt set them in two rows, six on a row, upon the pure table before the Lord" (Lev. 24:5-9).

Fine flour speaks of uniform perfection: no lumpiness or defect of any kind in the life or character of Jesus Christ. No matter how fine the flour is, man would hardly survive on raw flour; but most of us do well on baked goods. Even so, no one is saved by the perfect *life* of Christ; redemption rests on His atoning *death*. *Baking* connotes His suffering and death by which He redeemed us. Verily, Christ crucified is the True Bread from heaven (John 6:32, 33, 35, 41, 48, 50, 51, 58).

Cakes (Lev. 24:5), translated from the Hebrew word *challah* (# 2471 in Strong's Concordance), is "a cake (as usually punctured)." Young's Concordance defines it as "a perforated cake." The body of Christ was *punctured* fivefold on the cross.

The Shewbread was "hallowed bread" (1 Sam. 21:6), basically intended for priests only (Mt. 12:3, 4). In the New Testament true disciples "are an holy priesthood" (1 Peter 2:5), "a chosen generation, a royal priesthood" (2:9). For Christ "hath made us kings and priests unto God" (Rev. 1:6; 5:10). All born again Christians have access to the True Bread from heaven.

He upon whom the angels feed (Ps. 78:25) is the spiritual diet of all true believers. Both the Manna and the Shewbread typified Christ as the Bread from heaven. Although the Bible does not mention it, we have ample reason to believe that both were unleavened, typifying freedom from sin (Lev. 2:11; 10:12; Ex. 12:15; Mt. 16:6-12; Mark 8:15; 1 Cor. 5:6-8; Gal. 5:9).

III. THE GOLDEN LAMPSTAND
AND ITS BRANCHES

Exodus 25:31-39; 37:17-24; John 8:12

The Lampstand, having seven lamps but no candles, really was not a *candlestick*, as it is called in the King James Version. Like the Mercy Seat, it was of pure gold, depicting the full and perfect deity of Christ. There are no dimensions given, reminding us that deity knows no boundary and infinity has no limitations! A talent of gold, however, reminds us that Jesus paid an enormous price for our redemption. (At today's prices a talent of gold would exceed one-half million dollars!)

In addition to some ninety pounds of gold, imagine the labor investment. This ornate vessel of one shaft and six branches, with its twenty-two sets of buds, blossoms, and bowls, was hammered out of one piece (Ex. 25:36; 37:22). This was possible only by the power of God's Spirit, with whom He had endowed the workmen (Ex. 35:31-35).

Each branch had three sets of knops, flowers, and bowls like unto almonds, and the central stem (called the candlestick) had four sets (Ex. 25:32-35). Three stages of maturity (buds, blossoms, and mature almonds), all present at the same time, suggest everbearing and perpetual fruitfulness, possible only in Christ.

In the Revelation of Jesus Christ, John saw Jesus standing in the midst of seven candlesticks with seven stars in His right hand. The seven candlesticks were the seven churches (Rev. 1:12-20). Based on that and the following reasons, I assume that the Lampstand and its branches typify Christ and His Church.

When God "caused a deep sleep to fall upon Adam," He opened Adam's side, took out a rib, and *built*[2] a wife for Adam (Gen. 2:21-23). Now Adam "is the figure of him that was to come" (Rom. 5:14), and Eve typifies the church (Eph. 5:30-32). Adam's "deep sleep" typified the death of Christ.

The opening of Adam's side foreshadowed the piercing of Jesus' side, from which flowed "blood and water" (John 19:34). That is how Jesus obtained His Bride, the Church, "purchased with His own blood" (Acts 20:28) and sanctified "with the washing of water by the word" (Eph.5:26).

Moreover, "rivers of living water" spoke "of the Spirit which they that believe on him should receive" (John 7:38, 39). Notice, however, that the blood is mentioned first (John 19:34). No one can receive the Spirit until they have personally appropriated the blood of Christ to their own heart and life. They who have applied the Blood, and whom the Holy Spirit indwells and governs, are the Church that Christ has purchased.

The seven-branched Lampstand was supported by one Central Stem, suggestive of Christ Himself, "who walketh in the midst of the seven golden candlesticks" (Rev. 1:12—2:1). Of lamps there were seven (perfection), but of branches there were but six (the number of man—short of perfection)! "Six branches shall come out of the sides of it" (Ex. 25:32), most likely representing the Church totally dependent on Christ. "I am the vine, ye are the branches," speaks of Christ and His Church. The Lampstand is very much like the vine and its branches.

There were no windows, no natural light, nor any other lamp in the Tabernacle, except this Lampstand. Jesus is "the true light, which lighteth every man that cometh into the world" (John 1:9). "He was a burning and a shining light: and ye were willing for a season to rejoice in his light" (5:35).

He said, "As long as I am in the world, I am the light of the world" (9:5), but He expects His Church to be "the light of the world" (Mt. 5:14), from His ascension to the rapture.

If the branches prefigured the Church, then the beating of the branches spoke of a suffering Church as well as a suffering Saviour. Jesus explicitly told His disciples that the Church would suffer persecution, and that "some of you shall . . . be put to death" (Luke 21:12-17). Then He added, "But there shall not an hair of your head perish" (verse 18). No, that is not a contradiction! Martyrs who gave their lives for their faith in Christ have not perished. To die was their gain, their graduation and completeness (Rom. 8:36, 37). Their death bears fruit for eternity.

Isaiah pictures a sevenfold aspect of Christ that blends well with the Lampstand. "The spirit of the Lord shall rest upon him [the central stem that carries the branches and the lamps], the spirit of wisdom and understanding [each pair goes hand in hand], the spirit of counsel and might [second pair of branches], the spirit of knowledge and of the fear of the Lord [third pair]" (Isaiah 11:2). See illustration on page 79.

IV. OIL, TYPIFYING THE HOLY SPIRIT

A. OIL FOR THE LAMPS (Ex. 27:20, 21; Lev. 24:2-4)

This was pure olive oil obtained by beating. Does the Holy Spirit ever suffer? Yes. He can be grieved (Eph. 4:30), and grief is suffering. He can "be touched with the feeling of our infirmities" (Heb. 4:15) and "vexed" by our rebellion (Isa. 63:10). He is the Oil of Light, "to cause the lamp to burn always" (Ex. 27:20). Without the Spirit we have no light, and with Him there is no darkness.

B. OIL FOR ANOINTING (Ex. 30:22-33)

This holy ointment was made by a special formula, and strictly reserved for holy purposes such as consecrating the priests. It symbolizes the divine unction they needed to fulfill their duties.

Olive oil, without the spices, is also used for anointing the sick (James 5:13-16). Though oil does have healing properties, it is not the oil that does the healing. It portrays the healing that we trust the Lord to give, through the Holy Spirit, in response to the "prayer of faith."

QUESTIONS FOR DISCUSSION

1. What significant similarities has the Table with the Ark?
2. Both represent the same PERSON, but not the same PURPOSE.
3. How do they depict the deity of Christ, and the humanity?
4. Which one focuses especially on salvation and redemption?
5. Which one focuses on practical aspects of Christian living?
6. What does the Golden Crown tell us about the border?
7. What are the contrasts between the Shewbread and the Manna?
8. How does the Manna especially portray the deity of Christ?
9. How does the Shewbread emphasize His humanity and suffering?
10. How does the Lampstand foreshadow Christ and His Church?
11. Who did John see among the seven candlesticks (Rev. 1:12-20)?
12. What did Jesus say that those seven candlesticks represent?
13. What do knops, flowers, and bowls on the Lampstand signify?
14. What did Adam, the Lampstand, and Christ have in common?
15. What does the flowing of blood and water typify (John 19:34)?
16. By what energy did the lamps of the Lampstand "burn always"?

CHAPTER FOUR

THE CURTAINS AND COVERINGS
(four in number)
Exodus 26:1-14; 36:8-19

I. The LINEN CURTAIN, called THE TABERNACLE
Exodus 26:1-6

Only in this curtain is the "fine twined linen" given priority over the blue, purple, and scarlet colors (26:1). In all other parts of the Tabernacle the colors are named first. Linen is made from flax, a product of the soil. This curtain symbolizes the righteousness which Christ Incarnate wrought for us by His earthly ministry.

Egyptian linen was of super excellent quality, whiter than any fuller today could make it. The ability to make such quality was of the Lord, presumably in preparation for the Tabernacle. Some day, however, the Bride of Christ will be arrayed in linen superior to any earthly product. It will be "clean and white: for the fine linen is the righteousness of saints" (Rev. 19:8), cleansed and made holy by the blood of Christ.

One special feature in this curtain was several cherubim,

guardians of God's holiness, watching as it were, everything that went on in both parts of the Tabernacle. Cherubim were a warning to all who entered, to proceed with caution. They were indeed treading on holy ground.

This Fine Linen Curtain was composed of ten strips, each 28 cubits long, and four cubits wide. Five of these were coupled together into one section, and five into another section. Then the two sections were coupled together with one hundred loops of blue and fifty taches (buckles or clasps) of gold (Ex. 26:1-6).

While we do not try to *prove* anything by our typological numbers, the recorded facts do present interesting combinations. Some of them surely were more than mere coincidence. We agree that the fine linen was a product of earth (4), which was the width of each strip, and its quality was perfect (7). Quality (7), times the width (4), equals the length (28) of each strip. Only by grace (5) is righteousness obtained, and five coupled to five (grace upon grace!) equals ten (the number of completeness, ALL BY GOD'S GRACE THROUGH JESUS CHRIST OUR LORD!

Notice especially the fifty loops of blue [BLUE it had to be] on the edge of each section (26:4, 5), and the fifty taches of gold (v. 6) to couple the two sections together: "and it shall be one tabernacle." Forty-nine or fifty-one would have marred the type. Fifty was not an arbitrary number but one for which there is no substitute: 5 x 10 = GRACE COMPLETED.

"And ye shall hallow the fiftieth year, and proclaim liberty throughout all the land unto all the inhabitants thereof" (Lev. 25:10-24). Every fiftieth year was to be a Year of Jubilee. Debts were canceled, mortgages released, and captives set free. That is exactly what Jesus did for us (spiritually) on Calvary. That, indeed, was COMPLETE GRACE!

According to Luke, Jesus launched His preaching ministry in Nazareth by reading from Isaiah 61:1, 2.

"The Spirit of the Lord is upon me, because he hath anointed me to preach the gospel to the poor; he hath sent me to heal the brokenhearted, to preach deliverance to the captives, and recovering of sight to the blind, to set at liberty them that are bruised, to preach the acceptable year of the Lord" (Luke 4:18, 19).

Jesus stopped reading in the middle of a sentence (see Isa. 61:2), because "the day of vengeance" had not yet come. He had come "to preach the acceptable year of the Lord," salvation through His sacrifice on Calvary. At Calvary Jesus canceled our sin debt and set true believers free from slavery to Satan. That was all so beautifully illustrated by the Year of Jubilee, and is symbolized in this curtain by the fifty taches.

"Thou shalt hang up the veil under the taches" (Ex. 26:33). The veil and the taches both relate to Calvary, and it was God who specified their close proximity. When Jesus canceled the sin debt on Calvary, the veil in the Temple was rent (Mt. 27:51), offering free access to the throne of Grace (Heb. 4:16).

By God's redemptive grace (5) the fine linen of righteousness, "even the righteousness of God," is *imputed* to the believer *by faith* (Rom. 3:22-26; 4:22-24). Then God's enabling grace (5) *imparts* to believers the grace to "be *partakers* of the divine nature" (2 Peter 1:4) *by experience.* When the imputed and the imparted righteousness arc coupled together by the believer's faith and experience of Calvary *(fifty* taches), "it shall be one tabernacle" (Ex. 26:6) wherein God dwells. Then it is no longer you, but *"Christ in you,* the hope of glory" (Col. 1:27b).

II. THE GOATS' HAIR CURTAIN
Exodus 26:7-13

"And thou shalt make curtains of goats' hair to be a covering upon the tabernacle: eleven curtains shalt thou make . . . . And thou shalt couple five curtains by themselves, and six curtains by themselves" (Ex. 26:7, 9a). These two distinct sections suggest a double typological meaning.

A. *The Goats' Hair Curtain first of all typifies the sin of man, human failure, and confusion.* Adam and Eve had been created absolutely righteous and perfectly holy. They were as pure as the righteousness symbolized by the fine linen curtain. One sin ruined it all! Their righteousness was gone, and they were sin-scarred in spirit, soul, and body. The verdict, "Thou shalt surely die," became reality. It was the beginning of human failure and confusion.

To symbolize the dilemma, eleven is the appropriate number, and goats' hair the appropriate material. Goats have been used for deception. Rebekah used kid skins to deceive Isaac into mistaking Jacob for Esau (Gen. 27:11, 16). David's wife Michal used a goats' hair pillow to deceive Saul's messengers (1 Sam. 19:12-17). In the judgment of the nations (Mt. 25:31-46), those set on the left are called goats. So goats have been used to symbolize human failure and sin.

Six being the number of man, the six curtains coupled by themselves emphasize the fallen nature of man. Moses was told to "double the sixth curtain in the forefront of the tabernacle" (Ex. 26:9b). The doubled curtain hung down over the top of the Tabernacle Door, where it could always be plainly seen from the area of the brazen altar. This should remind us that, though our sins may be forgiven, our flesh is not eradicated. David's sin had been forgiven and his heart cleansed, yet he confessed, "My sin is ever before me" (Ps. 51:31). Like David, we have all been "shapen in iniquity" (v.5). We need repeated cleansing by the blood of Christ and constant grace to live victoriously.

The Goats' Hair Curtain is called "the tent" (Ex. 26:11, 12, 14). Our earthly bodies are the temporary tent in which we live. We may be redeemed by the blood of Christ and "have the firstfruits of the Spirit, [yet] even we ourselves groan within ourselves, waiting for the adoption, to wit, the redemption of our body" (Rom. 8:23). Funerals are reminders that these earthly tents are not yet redeemed. Our flesh must be controlled, but it will not be eradicated until it is vacated.

B. *The Goats' Hair Curtain also typifies Christ as our Sin Offering* (Isa. 53:10; 2 Cor. 5:21). The Bible specifies eleven occasions when goats were to be used for a sin offering (Lev. 4:22-26, 27-28; 9:3; Nu. 15:22-24; 28:11, 17, 22, 29; 29:5,

11, 16-38). In all of these cases goats typify Christ as our atonement, the ultimate and ONLY efficacious Sin Offering for man. God has made Christ who knew no sin, to be "an *offering* for sin" (Isa. 53:10), "that we might be made the righteousness of God in him" (2 Cor. 5:21).

Yes, the Greek word for "sin" in 2 Corinthians 5:21 is *hamartia*, translated *sin* 172 times in the New Testament. But Jesus "did no sin" (1 Peter 2:22), and He "knew no sin" (2 Cor. 5:21). He "is holy, harmless, undefiled, separate from sinners" (Heb. 7:26), "and in him is no sin" (1 John 3:5). Obviously, Jesus did not literally become sin but was made "an offering for sin" (Isa. 53:10), paying the price for our redemption.

The scapegoat was also used to make an atonement for Israel (Lev. 16:10), bearing "their iniquities unto a land not inhabited" (verses 20-22). Likewise Christ, our effectual Sin Offering, removes our sins from us "as far as the east is from the west." There is no justification for continuing in known sin!

"And thou shalt make *fifty* taches of brass, . . . and couple the tent together, that it may be one" (Ex. 26:9, 11). Five curtains (# of grace) coupled to six (# of man), rescue fallen man from human failure and chaos (typified by 11 curtains). As the fifty taches of brass coupled "the tent together, that it may be one," so Calvary (typified by the 50th Year) couples the redeemed (6) to their Gracious Redeemer (5) that they may be one! "As thou, Father, art in me, and I in thee, that they also may be one in us" (John 17:21).

III. THE COVERING OF RAMS' SKINS DYED RED

Exodus 26:14a

Rams were used for consecrating the priests for office, one for a burnt offering (Ex. 29:15-18), and one for the consecration (verses 19-22). For our sakes Jesus sanctified Himself (John 17:19) to be both our High Priest and our Sacrifice at the same time. No human priest could have qualified to officiate at that sacrifice.

"For such an high priest became us, who is holy, harmless, undefiled, separate from sinners, and made higher than the heavens; who needeth not daily, as those high priests, to offer up sacrifice, first for his own sins, and then for the people's: for this he did once, when he offered up himself . . . consecrated for evermore" (Heb. 7:26-28).

Jesus "made himself of no reputation, and took upon him the form of a servant, and was made in the likeness of men: and being found in fashion as a man, he humbled himself, and became obedient unto death, even the death of the cross" (Phil. 2:7, 8).

Rams' skins denote Christ, our Suffering High Priest, "consecrated for ever more." First He was our atoning sacrifice. Ever since He has been the "mediator between God and men" (1 Tim. 2:5). But rams' skins undyed were not sufficient. They had to be dyed red, obviously symbolizing the blood of Christ, without which there "is no remission" (Heb. 9:22).

IV. THE TOP COVERING OF BADGERS' SKINS (Ex. 26:14b)

What really were these "badgers' skins"? Adam Clarke says, "Few terms have afforded greater perplexity to critics and commentators than this." He thinks no animal is intended but a color, and names six colors that may be intended. Modern copy-righted translations use quite a variety of names, including both land and sea animals. Whatever the top covering was, it must have been a tough, durable leather that was also used for shoes (Ezek. 16:10). Surely it was non-porous, water repellent and weather resistant, protecting the beautiful interior for at least forty years. Protection was its purpose.

Exquisite beauty abounded on the inside of the Tabernacle, which the outside world never saw. The exterior concealed, protected, and safely preserved all that inner beauty. It withstood the burning heat of the sun, the pelting of the rain, and the beating of the storm. Does that not symbolize the torture, the ridicule, the shame, and the spitting that Jesus endured for our sake? His mutilated features had "no form nor comeliness; . . . no beauty that we should desire him" (Isa. 53:2).

There are no dimensions given for the two upper coverings. Dimensions set bounds, limitations, thus far and no further. But the cleansing power of Jesus' blood (typified by the Rams' Skins Dyed Red) is immeasurable. That unsightly, sun-tanned, weather-beaten leather covering may typify the boundless and immeasurable protection that believers have in Christ.

Non-Christians never see the inner beauty of Christ. They may see Him as an ordinary man (leather), or perhaps as a good man and a spiritual leader (fine leather). But looking deeper we find Christ to be the Blessed Redeemer, the atoning Sacrifice (Rams' Skins Dyed Red) by whom God can justly redeem fallen man from human failure and sin (Goats' Hair Curtain). Jesus Christ is the "righteousness of saints" (Ten Curtains of Fine Twined Linen), bringing home "to himself a glorious church, not having spot, or wrinkle, or any such thing; but that it should be holy and without blemish" (Eph. 5:27). Acceptable righteousness is available only through Christ (Rom. 3:22-26; 4:22-24; 10:3; Phil. 3:9). "Yea, he is altogether lovely. This is my beloved, and this is my friend" (S. of Sol. 5:16).

QUESTIONS FOR DISCUSSION

1. What, really, is "the righteousness of saints" (Rev. 19:8)?
2. How does it compare with Adam's original holiness?
3. How much disobedience did it take to ruin it all for Adam?
4. Is God more tolerant today than He was with Adam?
5. Why did the Goats' Hair Curtain cover every thread of Linen?
6. Why eleven curtains; and Goats' Hair for the chosen material?
7. How could six curtains coupled to five first symbolize sin, and then also symbolize Christ as an Offering for sin?

8. Well, what do Rams' Skins Dyed Red, and no dimensions, symbolize?
9. What, missing in the Goats' Hair, did the Rams' Skins supply?
10. Is there anything too hard for our Consecrated High Priest?
11. What do fifty taches of gold and fifty of brass typify?
12. How do gold and brass supplement and complement each other, their united symbolism doing what neither could do alone?
13. Of whatever hides the top cover consists, what major purpose does it serve, and whose greater service does it symbolize?
14. How does our experience prove our need of that very service?
15. What evidence have you had of that service in your life?

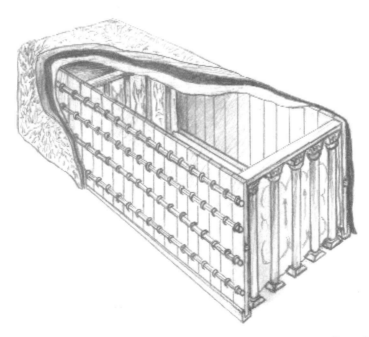

Showing both the Curtains and Coverings, as well as the Tabernacle Structure, discussed in Chapter Five.

CHAPTER FIVE

THE TABERNACLE STRUCTURE
Exodus 26:15-37; 36:20-38

(Boards, Bars, Sockets, Pillars of the Veil and the Door)

I. BOARDS "standing up," SOCKETS and BARS
Exodus 26:15-29

The first step to make boards is to cut down trees, sever them from their earthbound roots, and strip them of all their branches. Likewise, to be transformed from sinners into saints, we must be cut loose from our carnal roots and be stripped of every tentacle that reaches out to embrace this world's system.

We must fall at Jesus' feet and submit to spiritual surgery. Only then can we be upright members of Christ's body. We need a heart transplant, like God promised to Israel:

"From all your filthiness, and from all your idols, will I cleanse you. A new heart also will I give you, and a new spirit will I put within you: and I will take away the stony heart out of your flesh, and I will give you an heart of flesh" (Ezek. 36:25b, 26).

41

If the Tabernacle represents Christ and His Church on earth, then the boards must symbolize the members of His body, *standing upright* in Christ (*encased in gold*). What a blessed contrast to fallen man apart from Christ! "Dust thou art, to dust returnest [Gen. 3:19], was not spoken of the soul." [3] Instead, God has "made us accepted in [Christ] the beloved" (Eph. 1:6). In Him we are "fitly joined together" (4:16).

Every board was *ten* cubits long (responsibility *completed*) and 1½ cubits wide (*three* half-cubits, approved by the *Trinity*). Completeness is not in man but in Christ! Those boards symbolize a status of uniform perfection to which man of himself cannot attain, a status that is available ONLY in Christ.

The illustration below shows what makes the Tabernacle boards perfectly uniform in the eyes of God. The top line represents the perfection which God requires, and PROVIDES IN CHRIST. The naked arrows illustrate the SELF-righteous approach: "filthy rags" (Isa. 64:6); "measuring themselves by themselves, and comparing themselves among themselves" (2 Cor. 10:12). They simply lower their standard (broken line) to where they feel comfortable in themselves. Valid perfection is found only in Jesus Christ as illustrated by the four who are in Him. The shortest one of all represents a newborn babe in Christ. In Him he is reckoned as holy and as perfect as the tallest of all. In Christ, God sees him as already perfected, as having reached the upper

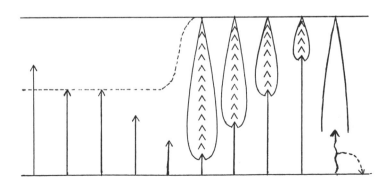

line. His taller brethren likewise see him, not as a hopeless runt, but as one whose perfection is in Christ, fully as perfect as a mature saint of God. We understand that the Tabernacle boards (each encased in gold) represent the members of Christ's body (Eph. 5:30). Each one is complete (ten cubits high), because Christ is their perfection.

The tallest of them received Christ in his youth. Through the grace and strength of Christ he has grown to where he now is. He knows full well that he has no perfection in himself, that it was the grace of God through Christ that brought him thus far, and that he is accepted ONLY in Christ (Eph. 1:6). Those little marks (∧) pointing upward represent holy aspirations for lifelong growth in Christ.

Those with aspiration marks represent Christians in various stages of growth, knowing that their salvation depends on ABIDING in Christ. By trusting Him they keep growing.

The fallen one had received Christ, but has now forsaken the crucified life and is "doing his own thing." Whether by living "after the flesh" (Rom. 8:13b), or seeking to be "justified by the law" (Gal. 5:4), he makes Christ "of no effect" in his life. His spiritual stature is buckling! The arms of Christ remain wide open, but by going his own way this person is about to plunge to his eternal ruin. Unless he repents he will find no place in the Tabernacle.

Apart from Christ, no one is complete and there are no two members alike. All perfection is in Christ. He alone can bridge the chasm from human imperfection "unto the measure of the stature of the fulness of Christ" (Eph. 4:13). In Him man is no longer known "after the flesh" (2 Cor. 5:16). In Christ we become "partakers of the divine nature" (2 Pet. 1:4). God sees believers as "complete in [Christ]" (Col. 2:10), "that ye may stand perfect and complete in all the will of God" (4:12b).

There were forty-eight boards in all, but the number forty-eight is not found. Instead, it says *twenty* boards on each side (ten doubled = dual completion). Jesus completed every responsibility toward God and man! At the west end there

West End

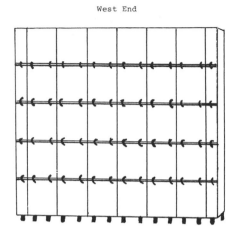

were *six* boards, plus *two* corner boards, obviously mitered around the corners, tying all three sides together: 6 (number of man) + 2 (union with Christ) = 8 (new beginning). Surely Christ "is become the head . . . of the corner" (Ps. 118:22).

Two (union with Christ) is the prominent number here (found thirteen times in Exodus 26:17-27 and ten times in 36:22-30). Believers in Christ (boards of wood overlaid with gold) yield their personal identity to identify with Him who is fully God yet fully Man. Union with Christ is indeed the secret of Life.

At registration, each soldier gave half a shekel of silver as atonement money. God said, "The rich shall not give more, and the poor shall not give less than half a shekel" (Ex. 30:13-15). The cost of atonement is the same for every soul.

Three thousand shekels make one talent, the weight of each socket (Ex. 38:25-27). Each board stood upon two sockets, which was the atonement money of twelve thousand men. Atonement is EXTREMELY COSTLY. See Psalm 49:7, 8 in NIV or in German.

These boards stood side by side, held firmly together by *five* bars (*grace*) all the way around. The bars were of shittim wood overlaid with gold, typical of the dual nature of Christ. "And he made the middle bar to shoot through the boards from the one end to the other" (Ex. 36:33), an appro-

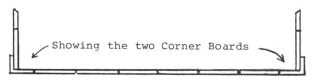

Showing the two Corner Boards

priate reminder of "Christ in you, the hope of glory" (Col. 1:27).

Both the middle bar and the corner boards raise a question as to the thickness of the boards. Josephus says "the thickness was four fingers."[4] Solid boards that thick, and $1\frac{1}{2} \times 10$ cubits} would have been extremely heavy. Some translations call them frames instead of boards. Perhaps they were hollow panels, with an interior framework to provide maximum strength with minimum weight. The dimensions of the corner boards and the "bar to shoot *through* the boards" would seem to require a thickness of at least three inches. See illustration of the corner boards.

At any rate, making boards that size (probably with hand tools and homemade glue) and bars 45 feet long from a tree whose maximum height is about 25 feet, demonstrates the marvel of their God-given ingenuity (Ex. 31:1-6).

According to Josephus the bars were in five-cubit sections, joined together by male-female couplings, "so fastened in their joints, that they held the whole firmly together."[5]

II. THE VEIL, ITS SILVER SOCKETS AND FOUR PILLARS
Exodus 26:31-33; 36:35-36

"Thou shalt make a veil of blue, and purple, and scarlet, and fine twined linen of cunning work: with cherubim shall it be made" (Ex. 26:31). The Bible does not say what the four prominent colors stand for, but we do know that Jesus more than matches all the symbolisms suggested for the colors. He really *is* the Heavenly One (blue), the Royal One (purple), the Suffering Servant (scarlet), and the Righteous One (fine [white] linen). All these colors were woven into the Veil, and the Bible tells us that the Veil represents Christ's flesh (Heb. 10:20).

Therefore it seems safe to assume that the colors denote

the attributes of Christ. No wonder the veil in the temple was rent in twain at the moment Christ died! By His death He consecrated for us "a new and living way" into the Holy of Holies, giving us access to the Blood-sprinkled Mercy Seat.

The rending of the Veil in the Temple shows God's interest in the meaning of His types and shadows. That Veil was probably four times as large and more than twice as thick as its predecessor in the Tabernacle, but that in no way mars the symbolism. The way to the Holy of Holies was closed, except on the Great Day of Atonement when "the high priest alone [entered with awesome caution] once every year, NOT WITHOUT BLOOD" (Heb. 9:7).

Violations were punishable by death. But on Calvary Christ opened "a new and living way" (Heb. 10:20), so that we are now invited to "come boldly unto the throne of grace, that we may obtain mercy, and find grace to help in time of need" (4:16).

This beautiful Veil, embroidered with cherubim, hung on *four* pillars of wood overlaid with gold, and standing in sockets of silver. Four (the number of earth) is the most appropriate number of pillars to represent Christ's life on earth and His death on Calvary. Then there is that significant rending of the temple Veil at the very moment that Jesus died!

The pillars of the Veil stood in sockets of silver, symbolizing the atonement Christ wrought on Calvary. The hooks of gold upon which the Veil hung suggest His constant support from heaven, even while hanging on the cross. For truly, "God was in Christ, reconciling the world unto himself" (2 Cor. 5:19).

III. THE DOOR, FIVE PILLARS, CHAPITERS AND FILLETS OF GOLD, AND SOCKETS OF BRASS
Exodus 26:36-37; 36:37-38

The Door (Tabernacle entrance) had a hanging of blue, purple, scarlet, and fine twined linen wrought with needlework. The design is not described, but the colors and fiber were just like the Veil. The pillars were wood overlaid with gold, the same as the pillars associated with the Veil. The three entrances (to the Court, to the Tabernacle, and to the Holy of Holies) all represent Christ, who is the Way, the Truth, and the Life.

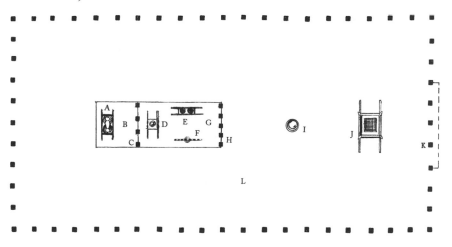

A	Ark of the Covenant	E	Table of Shewbread
B	Holy of Holies	F	Lampstand
C	The Veil	G	Sanctuary
D	Altar of Incense	H	Tabernacle Door

I	Brazen Laver
J	Brazen Altar
K	Gate of the Court
L	Court Yard

However, there are several significant contrasts. The door had no Cherubim, five pillars instead of four, brass sockets instead of silver, and the pillars were crowned with chapiters and fillets of gold (Ex. 36:38), of which we read nothing in connection with the Veil. Why the difference?

The Veil denotes the body of flesh in which Jesus suffered and died. In His earthly life and in His death He wore no golden crown, only a crown of thorns. At Calvary He was humiliated and "cut off" (Isa. 53:8) in the prime of His earthly life.

The *five* pillars at the Door were crowned with golden chapiters. Five is the number and Christ is the means of GRACE, freely extended to us. We are living in the era of grace. Jesus is no longer in the flesh, no longer humiliated. He is resurrected, ascended, crowned and glorified as Lord of all: hence five pillars appropriately crowned with golden chapiters!

Jesus is the Door to the sheepfold. Since He is the Gate, the Door, and the Veil we may safely assume that their primary role is to typify Him. Christ is the Alpha and Omega, the First and the Last, the Beginning and the End. He was the Architect of the Creation, and He will be the Engineer of the Consummation.

The pillars of the Door stand in five sockets of brass (brass typifies judgment). Once Jesus took our sins upon Himself and stood in judgment for us, but now and henceforth He will surely be our Judge (John 5:21-23a). And, "Behold, the Judge is *standing at the door!*" (James 5:9, NKJ).[6]

Five (the number of grace) sockets of brass (symbol of judgment) may seem like a contradiction. We find, however, that in the era of grace, grace abounds even in judgment. "For if we would judge ourselves, we should not be judged. But when we are judged, we are chastened of the Lord, that we should not be condemned with the world" (1 Cor.11:31-32). That is GRACE!

Remember that we do not use types to establish doctrine, but only to illustrate what the Bible clearly teaches.

QUESTIONS FOR DISCUSSION

1. If the boards of wood represent "members of his body" (Eph. 5:30), what part of the board represents Christ?
2. How do you account for the boards' perfect uniformity?
3. Why do the boards stand in sockets of silver, not of brass?
4. What is the typological evidence of their safe standing?
5. How could bars 45 feet long be made of shittim wood?
6. What does the Bible say that the Veil represents?
7. What features does the Veil have that the Door doesn't have?
8. Why do the pillars at the Veil stand in sockets of silver?
9. Why do the pillars at the Door stand in sockets of brass?
10. Why are the pillars at the Veil simply "cut off" at the top?
11. Why are the pillars at the Door crowned with gold chapiters?
12. Why do you think God was so specific about all these details?
13. Though we dare not be dogmatic about our conclusions, would God be pleased with our indifference about His specifics?
14. What symbolism do the Gate, Door, and Veil share in common?
15. Why do some who enter at the Gate, never get inside the Door?
16. What warning does that offer to casual "Christians"?

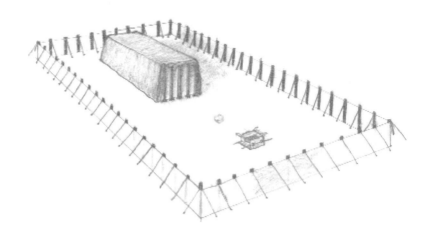

CHAPTER SIX

THE OUTER COURT, GATE, PILLARS AND HANG-INGS

Exodus 27:9-19; 38:9-20

I. THE COURT, PILLARS, SOCKETS, HANGINGS, HOOKS, PINS

Exodus 27:9-19

The outer Court separated the worship center from the out side world. Christians, you see, are in the world but not of the world (John 15:19; 17:14-16. They are set apart as God's purchased property and peculiar treasure, which of course means special discipline in keeping with their unique call-ing (Ex. 19:5; Amos 3:2; 2 Cor. 6:14-18; Eph. 5:11).

Around the court stood sixty pillars of brass—or wood overlaid with brass. The less than seventy-one talents of brass recorded in Exodus 38:29-31 would not have sufficed for the Laver, the grate and vessels of the altar, nearly two hundred tent pins, and sixty-five sockets plus sixty pillars of solid brass seven and a half feet high. The pillars are not even named among the items that used most of the brass.

Therefore we presume the court pillars were wood overlaid with brass.

Furthermore, wood typifies humanity. If the boards standing shoulder to shoulder represent the Church as the corporate Body of Christ, the pillars around the court may symbolize individual believers displaying Christ to the world. They are indeed upholding a fine linen hanging, and "fine linen is the righteousness of saints" (Rev. 19:8).

The Church stands in sockets of silver (atonement), but as individuals each one still stands alone, each in his own socket of brass (judgment). This illustrates what we already know, that in the final Judgment each person will stand alone, in a fixed position too late to change. Each one will be answerable for his own state of being. There will be no hiding behind another, no passing of blame to another.

Sixty brazen pillars, standing in *sixty* sockets of brass, were nevertheless crowned with silver (atonement). That is indeed a twelvefold multiplicity of grace (12 x 5 = 60). Yet the number sixty is not quoted at all. The pillars are enumerated as twenty on each side and ten at each end (2 x 20 plus 2 x 10 = 60). The court, 100 cubits long and 50 cubits wide, encircled with hangings 5 cubits high, abounded with multiples of 5 and 10, including 15, 20, 50, 60, and 100.

The hanging of fine twined linen was five cubits high all the way around the court. It reached from one end of the east gate, all the way around the court to the other end of the east gate. The gate, 20 cubits wide, left 15 cubits on each side of the gate to the corner, plus 100 cubits for each side and 50 cubits for the west end (2 x 15 = 30 + 250 = 280 cubits). That corresponds exactly with the embroidered fine linen curtain on top of the Tabernacle. The Linen Curtain consisted of ten strips, each 28 cubits long, which totaled exactly 280 cubits. For the numerical typology of that curtain, see Chapter Four.

There was not an ounce of gold in the outer court. The gold was all confined to the vessels, boards, pillars, and hooks either inside or attached to the Tabernacle structure, and well covered with the four Coverings upon it (Chapter Four).

The most prominent materials in the court were brass and wood. But at the top, above the fine linen hanging, were silver chapiters, fillets, and hooks, typifying atonement through Christ Incarnate, who gave His life in judgment for our sins and arose victorious over sin and death. The fillets of silver (atonement) carried the weight of the linen hanging (righteousness). You see, our righteousness in Christ depends wholly upon redemption through Him. Apart from redemption we have no righteousness.

The silver hooks at the top of the pillars were for the ropes that anchored the pillars to pins of brass (Ex. 27:19) driven into the ground like tent stakes. Each pillar was held securely erect. We too need to be anchored in our Lord Jesus Christ. Without Him we are as insecure as those pillars would be without an anchor.

The humanity, typified by the wood in the boards and pillars, may include believers as the body of Christ, while the gold and brass, respectively, may represent Christ as both our King and our Judge. He who gave Himself as a Suffering Servant [scarlet] and Consecrated High Priest [Rams' Skins Dyed Red] will just as surely be our Judge and our King!

The Bible does not specifically say on which side of the hanging the pillars stood. Some pictures show them outside the hanging, which mars the typology. Their purpose is to hold up that fine linen: "the righteousness of saints." One who is not "in Christ" has nothing to do with righteousness. If the pillars represent believers upholding Christ for the world to see, they must at least be on the inside. Otherwise they could not display Christ. Being crowned with silver chapiters denotes atonement, which cannot be obtained on the outside. Therefore it seems imperative that the pillars stand on the inside.

II. THE GATE AND ITS COLORS, BREADTH, AND HEIGHT
Exodus 27:16; 38:18, 19

"And for the gate of the court shall be an hanging of twenty cubits, of blue, and purple, and scarlet, and fine twined linen, wrought with needlework: and their pillars shall be four, and their sockets four"(27:16).

These were all included in the sixty pillars and sockets around the court, and apparently were identical with them.

The hanging of the Gate (representing Christ) was distinctively different from the pure white hanging of the court. In fact the Hebrew word *macak* (# 4539, pronounced maw-sawk) is used exclusively for the four-colored, embroidered linen used at the three entrances: the Gate, the Door, and the Veil. The word for the plain white hanging of the court is *qela'* (# 7050).

The Gate, the Door, and the Veil all bore the four prominent colors that portray various aspects and attributes of our Lord and Savior. Blue declares His heavenly origin (John 8:23), Purple His royalty (Rev. 19:16), Scarlet His suffering and death (Isa. 53), and Fine Linen His righteousness (1 John 2:29). Jesus towers above all others exclusively unique, as "holy, harmless, undefiled, separate from sinners, and made higher than the heavens" (Heb. 7:26).

The Gate, Door, and Veil are a threefold united emphasis that Jesus is truly the Way, the Truth, and the Life, and that no man ever comes to the Father but by Him (John 14:6). Each has its own unique emphasis as well. The Gate is only half as high as the Door and the Veil, but praise God it is twice as wide. The Altar (type of Calvary) is just inside the Gate. The invitation to Calvary redemption is wide open to one and all, as suggested by the double width. Our yards may be entered by way of a gate, but the house by way of a door (Truth). Not everything that enters at the gate continues into the house. See Mt. 13:41-42, 47-50.

The second passage way is the Door, only half as wide but twice as high as the Gate. The purpose and character of a door is twofold. It is designed to admit entrance and to prevent entrance. The same is true of Christ. He prevents the entrance of sin, and those who choose sin rather than the way of the cross cannot enter where Christ reigns. Some who enter the Gate by an outward profession are not willing to follow through with a crucified life. The closer one comes to the Lord, the more the path narrows. Only the narrow way leads to heaven; the broad way ever leads to hell.

The third passage way is through the Veil, which signifies the death of Christ, and tells us that we too must die to self before we can be His disciple (Mark 8:34-38; Luke 14:26-27). He who presently is the Door to the sheepfold will eventually be our Judge (Acts 10:42). Abiding crucified with Christ (Gal. 2:20) assures entrance through the Veil, the "new and living way." Refusing the crucified life is cause enough to prevent entrance when the Judge of all the earth calls His children home.

QUESTIONS FOR DISCUSSION

1. The Outer Court already provides separation from what?
2. Is "Outer Court" separation sufficient for total victory?
3. How many degrees of separation are shown in the Tabernacle?
4. Does the New Testament diminish or intensify our separation?
5. What symbols of divine judgment do you see in the Court?
6. Where does the evidence of judgment cease in the Tabernacle?
7. Is judgment from there on abandoned or intensified?
8. What in the Tabernacle replaces the prominence of brass?
9. Does that suggest more lenience or more holiness?
10. Why are the cherubim all in the Sanctuary and none outside?
11. What is the Biblical role and function of the cherubim?
12. Which effects the most reverence, brass, gold, or cherubim?
13. With whom and when does judgment begin, daily in life or once in death?
14. What do the pillars of the Court hold high for all to see?
15. Since the Court pillars are crowned with silver (atonement), why do they still stand in sockets of brass?
16. Why is the silver on the pillars of the Court confined to the chapiters at the very top, while in the Tabernacle it is confined to the sockets on which the boards stand?

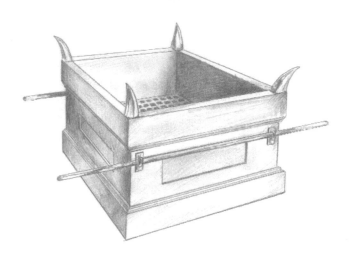

CHAPTER SEVEN

THE BRAZEN ALTAR AND THE BRAZEN LAVER

I. THE BRAZEN ALTAR

Exodus 27:1-8; 38:1-7

"And thou shalt make an altar of shittim wood, five cubits long, and five cubits broad; and the altar shall be foursquare: and the height thereof shall be three cubits. And thou shalt make the horns of it upon the four corners thereof: his horns shall be of the same: and thou shalt overlay it with brass" (Ex. 27:1,2).

This Altar was the one place where all their sacrifices were to be offered. Obviously it represents Calvary, because God said if anyone offers a sacrifice, "and bringeth it not unto the door of the tabernacle of the congregation, to offer an offering unto the Lord . . .; blood shall be imputed unto that man; he hath shed blood; and that man shall be cut off from among his people" (Lev. 17:3, 4, 5, 6, 9). Of course God had a valid reason for every stipulation, and He had a reason for this. ANY SUBSTITUTE FOR CALVARY IS SPIRITUALLY FATAL!

God Himself chose not only the place and the sacrifice (Gen. 22:2; Ex. 20:24b; Dt. 12:5, 11, 14, 18, 26; 14:23-25; 16:2, 6, 7, 15, 16), but also the material and the dimensions for the altar. There were no arbitrary options.

The wood, typifying humanity, reminds us that Christ became Man for the express purpose of experiencing our infirmities, and "to minister, and to give his life a ransom for many" (Mark 10:45). "For we have not an High Priest which cannot be touched with the feeling of our infirmities: but was in all points tempted like as we are, yet without sin" (Heb. 4:15).

The length and breadth, *five* cubits foursquare, reminds us of the grace of God equally available to all mankind. Horns illustrate power (2 Chron. 18:10; Hab. 3:4). Horns on every corner of this altar probably symbolize the power of the blood, available and equally efficacious for all people worldwide.

The Bible tells us "that God [the Father] was in Christ, reconciling the world unto himself" (2 Cor. 5:19), and that Christ "through the eternal Spirit offered himself without spot to God" (Heb. 9:14). This tells us that all three Persons of the Holy Trinity were involved at Calvary. The Altar being *three* cubits high may be a hint of the Trinity's involvement.

The wood and the horns being overlaid with brass typifies judgment.   Calvary was a manifestation of God's necessary judgment upon sin. The sinless Son of God, "the Just for the unjust" (1 Pet. 3:18), was the only Being in the universe qualified to offer a sacrifice sufficient for our atonement!

The net, or grate, was of solid brass (no wood), therefore capable of bearing the heat of the fire. "And thou shalt put it *under* the compass of the altar beneath, that the net may be even to the *midst* of the altar" (Ex. 27:5). Mid-altar may denote His inner anguish, when Jesus cried, "My God, my God, why hast thou forsaken me?" (Mt. 27:46). Halfway down puts the grate to the same height as the Table and the Ark. Table fellowship and the Mercy Seat were both made possible through Calvary.

"Seven days thou shalt make an atonement for the altar, and sanctify it; and it shall be most holy" (Ex. 29:37). Seven days of sanctification indicates the importance of this Altar.

II. THE BRAZEN LAVER

Exodus 30:17-21; 38:8

"Thou shalt also make a laver of brass, and his foot also of brass, to wash withal: and thou shalt put it between the tabernacle of the congregation and the altar, and thou shalt put water therein" (Ex. 30:17).

We believe the Laver typifies Jesus Christ, who "was ordained of God to be the *Judge* of quick and dead" (Acts 10:42). "For the Father judgeth no man, but hath committed all judgment unto the Son" (John 5:22). Solid brass with no wood, and with no dimensions given, beautifully portrays His divinely inspired judgments as totally immune from human limitations.

It is significant that the brass for the Laver was obtained from "the looking glasses of the women" (Ex. 38:8). The Bible likens God's Word to a mirror (James 1:22-25). God expects us to use His Word to judge and cleanse our own walk of life, even as a mirror is used for outward grooming. "For if we would judge ourselves we should not be judged" (1 Cor. 11:31).

The water in the Laver undoubtedly typifies the Word of God, by which all men will ultimately be judged. The Word of God is called *judgments* eighteen times in Psalm 119. Jesus said, "He that rejecteth me, and receiveth not my words, hath one that judgeth him: the word that I have spoken, the same shall judge him in the last day" (John 12:48). Hereby Jesus assures us that He will judge according to His written Word! Water used in ceremonial cleansing typifies the Word, and that is how it was used in the Laver.

> "For Aaron and his sons shall wash their hands and their feet thereat: when they go into the tabernacle of the congregation, they shall wash with water, that they die not; or when they come near to the altar to minister, to burn offering made by fire unto the Lord: so shall they wash their hands and their feet, that they die not: and it shall be a statute for ever . . . throughout their generations" (Exodus 30:19-21).

The first step in consecrating the priests was for Moses to wash them with water (Ex. 29:4; 40:12; Lev. 8:6). This ceremonial bathing was delegated to Moses, but it certainly symbolized a deeper cleansing, which only God could do. Christ likewise sanctifies and cleanses the Church "with the washing of **WATER** by the **WORD**" (Eph. 5:26). "Now ye are clean through the **WORD** which I have spoken unto you" (John 15:3). This is the spiritual bath to which Jesus referred when He said to Peter, "He that is washed [*louo*-bathed completely] needeth not save to wash [*nipto*-wash only a part, such as] his feet" (John 13:10).

The feet-washing service, as commanded in John 13:1-17, certainly takes on a deeper meaning the moment we see the water as typifying the Word of God. Stooping down and washing my brother's feet symbolizes a readiness to render menial, humble service to my brethren. But that is barely half of the story!

Our feet symbolize our walk of life, and the water the Word of God. To extend my bare feet to my brother symbolizes my willingness to lay my life bare before my brethren and have them use the Word of God to help me cleanse and improve my walk of life. I'd better mean it lest I play the hypocrite. Then, as I wash my brother's feet, I symbolize my willingness to use the Word to help him improve his walk of life. To do that in a brotherly way requires a far deeper humility than to simply wash his feet and dry them with a towel!

There are instances where the WORD is called WATER. "Except a man be born of **water** [the **Word**] and of the Spirit, he cannot enter the kingdom of God" (John 3:5). Obviously "the word of truth" is the seed by which the Father begat us (James 1:18). The gospel was the seed by which Paul had begotten the Corinthians (1 Cor. 4:15). For we are "born again, not of corruptible seed, but of incorruptible, by the **word** of God which liveth and abideth for ever" (1 Pet. 1:23). The Word of God does the "washing of regeneration" by which the Spirit renews us (Titus 3:5). And "the washing of **water** by the **word**" (Eph. 5:26) continues the process of progressive sanctification as long as we live. So the WATER in John 3:5 is the WORD.

Observe four great doctrines illustrated by the Altar:
Atonement: Lev. 17:11, 14; Heb. 9:22
Redemption: Gal. 3:13; Eph. 1:7; Col. 1:14; Titus 2:14
Justification: Rom. 3:24-26; 5:1, 2
Initial Sanctification: Heb. 10:10, 14; 1 Cor. 1:30
Observe four great doctrines illustrated by the Laver:
Regeneration: John 3:5; 1 Cor. 4:15; Titus 3:5; James 1:18;
1 Peter 1:23
Illumination: Psalm 119:105, 130; John 1:1, 9
Self-examination: 1 Cor. 11:28; James 1:22-25
Progressive Sanctification: 2 Cor. 3:18; Eph. 5:25-27

WARNING

"Behold therefore the *goodness* and *severity* of God: on them which fell [and did not repent], severity; but toward thee, goodness, *if thou continue in his goodness:* otherwise thou also shalt be cut off" (Romans 11:22).

"For the time is come that judgment must begin at the house of God: and if it first begin at us, what shall the end be of them that obey not the gospel of God? And if the righteous scarcely be saved, where shall the ungodly and sinner appear?" (1 Peter 4:17-18).

While the Laver and its cleansing water denote progressive sanctification for faithful believers, its brass also symbolizes the inevitable judgment of all apostates. Both of the verses just quoted solemnly warn us that judgment begins with God's people, but is intensified against apostates. To abide in Christ we need to be crucified with Him (Gal. 2:20) by faith; and progressive sanctification is the barometer of our faith.

QUESTIONS FOR DISCUSSION

1. What aspect of Jesus' ministry is typified by this Altar?
2. What may be the significance of the dimensions?
3. Why was it so offensive to offer sacrifices elsewhere?
4. For what typological purpose was the Altar framed with wood?
4. For what specific purposes had Jesus become fully Man?
5. What symbolism do the four horns and their location portray?
6. What important message do we get from the overlaying brass?
7. Why was it important for the Altar to be next to the Gate?
8. How many days did they sanctify the altar?
9. What official functions of Jesus does the Laver foreshadow?
10. What does total absence of wood and dimensions suggest?
11. From what did they obtain the brass to make the Laver?
12. How is the Word of God like a mirror? How is it like brass?
13. Do we "reinterpret" a mirror if we don't like what we see?
14. What is the Standard by which Jesus will judge the world, AND US?
15. What does water used in ceremonial cleansing typify?
16. How should that affect our appreciation for ceremonial washing?
17. For what precaution did God say the priests should wash?
18. What application does that have for us today?

CHAPTER EIGHT

THE HOLY GARMENTS OF THE HIGH PRIEST

I. THE EPHOD

Exodus 28:4-7; 39:1-4

"And they shall make the ephod of gold, of blue, and of purple, of scarlet, and of fine twined linen, with cunning work. It shall have two shoulder pieces thereof joined at the two edges thereof; and so it shall be joined together" (Ex. 28:6, 7).

"And they did beat the gold into thin plates, and cut it into wires, to work it in the blue, and in the purple, and in the scarlet, and in the fine linen, with cunning work" (Ex. 39:3).

Only in the Ephod, the Curious Girdle of the Ephod, and the Breastplate of Judgment do we find gold woven into any of the fabric connected with the Tabernacle. Review again the symbolism of the gold, blue, purple, scarlet, and the fine twined linen (page 13). Notice how this combination depicts the deity, the heavenly origin, the royalty, the suffering, and the spotless righteousness of Jesus Christ, in that order.

Observe also that "it shall have the *two* shoulder pieces thereof *joined* at the *two* edges thereof; and so it shall be *joined together*" (28:7). *Joining together* was the very purpose of the priesthood!

God had a definite purpose in the naming of Levi. "When the Lord saw that Leah was hated, he opened her womb: but Rachel was barren" (Gen. 29:31). While Rachel suffered for want of a son, Leah suffered for want of love. At the birth of her third son she exclaimed hopefully, "Now this time my husband will be *joined unto me*, because I have born him three sons: therefore was his name called Levi" (29:34), meaning *joined unto*.

The Levites typified the Church in many ways (see Chapter Twelve). They were *joined unto* Aaron (Nu.18:2, 4), a typological figure of the Church *joined unto* Christ, their spiritual Head. Furthermore, even after the Northern Kingdom had fallen, God spoke of a time when Israel would come and together with Judah would seek the Lord, to be *joined unto* Him.

> "In those days, and in that time, saith the LORD, the children of Israel shall come, they and the children of Judah together, going and weeping: they shall go and seek the LORD their God. They shall ask the way to Zion with their faces thitherward, saying, Come, and let us *join ourselves* to the LORD in a perpetual covenant that shall not be forgotten" (Jer. 50:4, 5).

Evidently God had several reasons to prescribe a two-piece ephod, *joined together* on the shoulders, symbolizing the role of Jesus Christ the eternal High Priest joining man to God.

II. THE CURIOUS GIRDLE OF THE EPHOD

Exodus 28:8; 39:5

> "And the curious girdle of the ephod, which is upon it, shall be of the same, ... even of gold, of blue, and purple, and scarlet, and fine twined linen" (28:8).

Moses "girded [Aaron] with the curious girdle of the ephod, and bound it [the ephod] unto him therewith" (Lev. 8:7b).

Binding the Ephod securely upon the high priest seems to have been the only physical purpose of this girdle. It did not reinforce or strengthen the loins of the wearer as *girdles* are intended to do (Ps. 65:6; 93:1b). It did, however, indicate readiness for service, which is another purpose for being girded (Luke 12:35-37; John 13:4, 5). And since the gold, blue, purple, scarlet, and fine twined linen all represent the superior attributes of Christ, it may well typify His readiness and strength to meet our every need. His strength never fails!

Also upon the shoulders of the Ephod were two onyx stones. Engraved on each stone were the names of six tribes of Israel, according to their birth (Ex. 28:9-12). The high priest daily bore those names on his shoulders before the Lord. Shoulders, being places of strength, remind us that Christ, our strong and faithful High Priest, will never let us down.

III. THE BREASTPLATE OF JUDGMENT

Exodus 28:15-21; 39:8-21

"And thou shalt make the breastplate of judgment with cunning work; after the work of the ephod thou shalt make it; of gold, of blue, and of purple, and of scarlet, and of fine twined linen, shalt thou make it. Foursquare it shall be being doubled; a span shall be the length thereof, and a span shall be the breadth thereof. And thou shalt set in it settings of stones, even four rows of stones: [three in each row] . . . and the stones shall be with the names of the children of Israel, twelve, . . . , according to the twelve tribes" (Ex. 28:15-21).

With its twelve precious stones the Breastplate is obviously the most costly and possibly the most significant of all the garments. It heads the list in 28:4. Apparently each stone had its own unique significance. Some writers define each one, perhaps correctly. But I fail to find any extensive descriptions in the Bible, and my knowledge of precious stones is too limited to attempt an explanation of their symbolism.

Notice, however, that each name was engraved twice (once on an onyx stone and once on a stone set in the Breastplate). This suggests what God later declared through Isaiah, that He would never forget His people (Isa. 49:15, 16). John saw the names of the twelve tribes written on the gates of the holy city that descended out of heaven from God (Rev. 21:10-12).

The Breastplate was securely fastened with four golden chains. Two of them were anchored to the shoulder pieces and two to the Curious Girdle, "that the breastplate be not loosed from the ephod." In His intercessory ministry, Christ always bears the names of God's children on His heart.

Notice that the word *two* (the number of fellowship and of union with Christ) occurs twelve times in Exodus 28:23-27 and thirteen times in 39:16-20. That's twenty-five times in ten verses! Union with Christ is the sinner's Life Line and the Christian's Anchor. It's a major theme in Tabernacle Study.

The Breastplate was a span long and wide, foursquare being doubled (28:16), or folded up forming a pouch. "And thou shalt put in the breastplate of judgment the Urim and Thummim; and they shall be upon Aaron's heart, when he goeth in before the Lord: and Aaron shall bear the judgment of the children of Israel upon his heart before the Lord continually" (28:30; Lev. 8:8).

Urim and Thummim are defined as lights and perfections, respectively. We are not told exactly how God revealed His will through the Urim and Thummim, but evidently it left no question in the minds of those who used them properly. After King Saul had turned from the Lord, "the Lord answered him not, neither by dreams, nor by Urim, nor by prophets" (1 Sam.28:6), and Saul knew that God was not answering him (28:15).

Urim and Thummim were a combination that represented God's perfect balance: balancing perception with forbearance, justice with pardon, judgment with mercy. "God is light, and in him is no darkness at all" (1 John 1:5b). "He is the Rock, his work is perfect: for all his ways are judgment: a God of truth and without iniquity, just and right is he" (Dt. 32:4). Jesus Christ is "the true Light, which lighteth every man that cometh into the world" (John 1:9).

All the perfections of God are manifested in Christ. He could well say, "He that hath seen me hath seen the Father" (John 14:9). "For in him dwelleth all the fullness of the Godhead bodily" (Col. 2:9). "In whom are hid all the treasures of wisdom and knowledge" (Col. 2:3). "Who being the brightness of his glory, and the express image of his person" (Heb. 1:3). In Christ we have the *lights* and the *perfections* of which Urim and Thummim were only a foreshadow.

IV. THE ROBE OF THE EPHOD ALL OF BLUE

Exodus 28:31-35: 39:22-26

"And thou shalt make the robe of the ephod all of blue. And there shall be an hole in the top of it, in the midst thereof: it shall have a binding of woven work round about the hole of it, as it were the hole of an habergeon, that it be not rent. And beneath upon the hem of it thou shalt make pomegranates of blue and of purple, and of scarlet, round about the hem thereof; and bells of gold between them round about: a golden bell and a pomegranate, a golden bell and a pomegranate, upon the hem of the robe round about" (28:31-34).

The Hebrew word here translated robe is found only 19 times in the Old Testament. Job, recalling the respect he once enjoyed, said, "My judgment was as a *robe* and a diadem" (Job 29:14b). Job apparently lived about the time of Abraham. The next ten occurrences refer to this robe of blue (Ex. 28:4 through Lev. 8:7), and Isaiah speaks of the robe of righteousness. Otherwise robes in the Old Testament were confined to kings and princes.

This Robe of Blue pointed to the Heavenly Prince, the coming "KING of Kings." I suspect it may have been seamless, like the coat of Jesus (John 19:23). At least it was made "of woven work, . . . [with] an hole in the midst of the robe" (39:22, 23).

Another special feature of the Robe was the full circle of golden bells and pomegranates around the hem. Pomegranates of blue, purple, and scarlet, in addition to the symbolism of the three colors, denote our Lord's fruitfulness on earth. As for the bells, "his sound shall be heard when he goeth in unto the holy place before the Lord, and when he cometh out, THAT HE DIE NOT" (Ex. 28:35).

The bells were meant to be heard when the high priest went in or came out of the Holy Place. Whenever I read Psalm 24:7-10, I visualize the joy bells in heaven ringing when our risen Lord, "The Lord strong and mighty," ascended back to heaven! When I read that "the Lord himself shall descend from heaven with a shout, with the voice of the archangel, and with the trump of God," then I wonder whether those golden bells were not a modest foreshadowing of the sounds that were heard when the King of Glory ascended back to heaven, and of the "SHOUT" when He comes again to take His Bride with Him to heaven.

I read on, "And the dead in Christ shall rise first: then we which are alive and remain shall be caught up together with them in the clouds, to meet the Lord in the air: and so shall we ever be with the Lord" (1 Thess. 4:16, 17). Then I wonder, *Is that why, in his second round (24:9-10), the Psalmist added "The Lord of hosts," to "The Lord strong and mighty (v.8)?* His next return HOME will not be a solo flight! He will take with Him a HOST of redeemed believers.   LET'S NOT MISS IT!

V. THE LINEN COAT: and VI. THE LINEN MITRE

"And thou shalt embroider the coat of fine linen, and thou shalt make the mitre of fine linen, and thou shalt make the girdle of needlework" (Ex. 28:39).

"And they made coats of fine linen of woven work for Aaron, and for his sons, and a mitre of fine linen, and goodly bonnets of fine linen, and linen breeches of fine twined linen, and a girdle of fine twined linen, of blue, and purple, and scarlet, of needlework; as the Lord commanded Moses" (Ex. 39:27-29).

Aaron's linen coat and girdle apparently were identical

with those worn by his sons. His headgear was a mitre while those of his sons are called bonnets. Both are Old Testament symbols of reverence before God, but the difference between the two is not clear to me. Aaron and his sons always wore the fine linen breeches, "that they bear not iniquity, and die"(28:42,43).

VII. THE PLATE OF PURE GOLD

Exodus 28:36-38; 39:30,31

"And thou shalt make a plate of pure gold, and grave upon it, like the engravings of a signet, HOLINESS TO THE LORD. And thou shalt put it on a blue lace, that it may be upon the mitre; upon the forefront of the mitre it shall be. And it shall be upon Aaron's forehead, that Aaron may *bear the iniquity of the holy things*, which the children of Israel shall hallow in all their holy gifts; and it shall always be upon his forehead, that they may be accepted before the Lord"(Ex.28:36-38).

By the above statement it is evident that the most holy things man can do are nevertheless tainted by our fallen nature, so that our High Priest, the Lord Jesus Christ, must bear the iniquity of our holy things. That Plate of Gold on Aaron's forehead was symbolic of Christ bearing with us, even with our very best intentions, gifts, and prayers. These are acceptable to God only by virtue of the shed blood of Christ. That is why Moses and the high priests "sprinkled with blood both the tabernacle, and all the vessels of the ministry" (Heb. 9:21) at least every year. The very best worship we can offer is acceptable only by virtue of the blood of Christ!

WARNING

"And when the king came in to see the guests, he saw there a man which had not on a wedding garment: and he saith unto him, Friend, how camest thou in hither not having a wedding garment? And he was speechless. Then said the king to the servants, Bind him hand and foot, and take him away, and cast him into outer darkness; and there shall be weeping and gnashing of teeth. For many are called, but few are chosen" (Mt. 22:11-14).

This would-be guest was probably wearing a beautiful suit of his own choosing. He may have looked with disdain upon the wedding garment which the king had chosen and freely supplied. His rejection of royal generosity was an insult to the king, as indicated by the consequences.

The High Priest's holy garments should remind us that the imputed righteousness of Jesus Christ (Rom. 4:8, 22-25) is the only garment in which we can be admitted to the wedding supper of the Lamb. The fig leaf garments of good works will never do! Faith in the blood of Christ is the only righteousness we can claim.

QUESTIONS FOR DISCUSSION

1. What was the basic purpose of the priesthood?
2. Why was the Ephod in two pieces, then joined together?
3. What does the name Levi mean?
4. Unto whom were the Levites to be joined?
5. To whom must we be joined to obtain salvation?
6. What three items had gold woven into their fabric?
7. Whom and what does each color and fabric typify?
8. What typological value do you see in the Curious Girdle?
9. What do the names on the priests' shoulders suggest?
10. What is suggested by their names borne on his bosom?
11. Where else does the Bible say those names are written?
12. What attribute of Christ is typified by the Urim and Thummim?
13. Why did the High Priest wear a Robe all of Blue?
14. What mean those golden bells and pomegranates on the hem?
15. What three garments were the same for all the priests?
16. What did the mitre and the bonnets signify?
17. How has the Headship of Christ affected this principle?
18. What does that Plate of Pure Gold suggest to us today?

CHAPTER NINE

THE CONSECRATION OF THE PRIESTS

Exodus 29:1-37; 40:12-16; Leviticus 8:1-36

"And the Lord spake unto Moses, saying, Take Aaron and his sons with him, and the garments, and the anointing oil, and a bullock for the sin offering, and two rams, and a basket of unleavened bread; and gather thou all the congregation together unto the door of the tabernacle of the congregation. And Moses did as the Lord commanded him; and the assembly was gathered together unto the door of the tabernacle of the congregation" (Lev. 8:1-4).

I. THE WASHING

Exodus 29:4; 40:12; Leviticus 8:5, 6

"And Moses said unto the congregation, This is the thing which the Lord commanded to be done. And Moses brought Aaron and his sons, and washed them with water" (Lev. 8:5, 6).

The initial washing was the first ceremonial act connected with consecrating the priests. Obviously it typified the New Testament "washing of regeneration, and renewing of the Holy Ghost" (Titus 3:5), which only God can do. God had told Moses that Aaron "shall be thy spokesman to the people: . . . and thou shalt be to him *instead of God*" (Ex. 4:16). Therefore Moses, as God's proxy, needed to do that washing.

(This initial bathing coincides with how Jesus explained the feet-washing service to Peter. "He that is washed [*louo*] needeth not save to wash [*nipto*] his feet, but he is clean every whit" (John 13:10). Jesus used two different Greek words: louo, meaning a complete bath [in this case, the washing of regeneration]; and *nipto*, meaning to wash only a part, like the hands or feet washed ceremonially, as He was doing for Peter.)

Leviticus 8 says nothing about the linen breeches without which the priests could not come near the altar. The breeches, God had said, "shall be upon Aaron, and upon his sons, when they come in unto the tabernacle of the congregation, or when they come near unto the altar to minister in the holy place; that they bear not iniquity, and die: it shall be a statute for ever unto him and his seed after him" (Ex. 28:43).

Ever since the fall of man, God wants the human body to be well clothed. Although their linen coats reached to their ankles, wearing the linen breeches appears to have been a life or death matter for the priests. Apparently Moses washed Aaron and his sons while they wore their breeches.

Then Moses clothed them. God Himself had clothed Adam and Eve, and here Moses did likewise, clothing them piece by piece. He *put* upon Aaron the coat, *girded* him with the girdle, *clothed* him with the robe, *put* the ephod upon him, *girded* him with the curious girdle, *put* the breastplate upon him, *put* the Urim and Thummim into the breastplate, *put* the mitre upon Aaron's head and *put* the golden plate upon his forehead (Lev. 8:7-9).

Six times he *put*; twice he *girded*; once he *clothed*. Every item and every act had its own unique significance, representing something that man cannot do for himself, but that God does for His children through our High priest, the Lord Jesus Christ.

II. THE ANOINTING

Leviticus 8:10-12

"And Moses took the anointing oil, and anointed the tabernacle and all that was therein, and sanctified them. And he sprinkled thereof upon the [brazen] altar seven times, and anointed the altar and all his vessels, both the Laver and his foot, to sanctify them" (Lev. 8:10-11).

The Tabernacle, and all that was therein and in the outer court, were anointed with oil: and all the vessels were sanctified. Only the brazen altar was sprinkled in addition to the anointing, and that seven times. That altar denotes Calvary!

"And he poured of the anointing oil upon Aaron's head, and anointed him, to sanctify him. And Moses brought Aaron's sons, and put coats upon them, and girded them with girdles, and put bonnets upon them; as the Lord commanded Moses" (8:12-13).

There are five passages (Ex. 28:41; 30:30; 40:15; Lev. 7:35, 36; Nu.3:3) that sound as though the sons were to be anointed as well as Aaron. Three others (Ex.29:7; 40:13; Lev. 8:12, 13) speak of anointing Aaron without mentioning the sons. Henry W. Soltau concludes that the anointing was "confined to Aaron, a type of the Messiah, the Christ, the Anointed One. The anointing of Aaron's sons was included in the anointing of Aaron himself."[7] He thinks Exodus 40:15 points to Aaron's successors after his death. I have no definite answer. We do not find that Eleazer was further anointed with oil when he became high priest (Nu. 20:24-29).

III. THE SIN OFFERING

Exodus 29:10-14; Leviticus 8:14:17

Prior to the consecration of Aaron, Israel had no high priest. Moses continued to perform all the official duties. "And he brought the bullock for the sin offering: and Aaron and his sons laid their hands upon the head of the bullock for the sin offering" (Lev. 8:14).

Exodus 29:10 is the first mention of laying hands on the head of an animal to be offered. This is a ceremonial act representing a transfer of one's sins to the head of a vicarious victim. Immediately after that transfer, Moses slew the bullock, "took the blood, and put it upon the horns of the altar . . ., purified the altar, and poured the blood at the bottom of the altar, and sanctified it, to make reconciliation upon it" (v.15).

Moses purified and sanctified the altar so that upon it he could make reconciliation for Aaron and his sons. The sin offering was essential to reconcile, sanctify, and purify the priests. Moses burned all the fat, the caul, and the two kidneys of the sin offering upon the altar. "But the bullock, and his hide, his flesh, and his dung, he burnt with fire without the camp: as the Lord commanded Moses" (Lev. 8:16, 17).

This appears to have been the first sin offering of its kind. Exodus 29 gives the initial instructions for it, and Leviticus was written *after* the priests were consecrated. The sin offering for a priest was to be a bullock (Lev. 4:3). "And no sin offering whereof any of the blood is brought into the tabernacle of the congregation to reconcile withal in the holy place, shall be eaten: it shall be burnt in the fire"(Lev. 6:30). The sin offering, portraying the cost of sin, was not a sweet savor unto God, and was to be burned with fire without the camp.

IV. THE RAM FOR THE BURNT OFFERING

Exodus 29:15-18; Leviticus 8:18-21

The Burnt Offering was the usual offering from the time of Abel. It signified God's acceptance of the offerer by virtue of and in anticipation of the shed blood of Christ, "wherein he hath made us accepted in the beloved [Son]" (Eph. 1:6b). For the consecration of the priests, the Burnt Offering was to be a ram (Ex. 29:15-18).

Moses "brought the ram for the burnt offering: and Aaron and his sons laid their hands on the head of the ram" (Lev.8:18). They identified with the victim, and claimed

God's promise of acceptance by virtue of the blood! And Moses killed the ram, sprinkled the blood upon the altar round about, cut the ram in pieces. Then "he washed the inwards and the legs in water; and Moses burnt the whole ram upon the altar: it was a burnt sacrifice for a sweet savour, and an offering made by fire unto the Lord" (vv.19-21). The Burnt Offering was a sweet savor.

Washing the inwards and the legs before burning them on the altar was a standard requirement for burnt offerings (Lev. 1:9). The inwards symbolize one's inner being, nature, affections and attitudes; while the legs typify our walk of life. After being redeemed by the blood of Christ, we need also to be sanctified and cleansed progressively "with the washing of water by the word" (Eph. 5:26), to be acceptable unto God as a sweet savor. Faith without fruit is a barren claim!

V. THE RAM OF CONSECRATION

Exodus 29:19-28; Leviticus 8:22-30

These are lengthy passages. Please follow in your Bible to understand the consecration. Moses brought the Ram of Consecration. Aaron and his sons, in acknowledgement of their guilt and their need, identified with the victim by laying their hands upon its head. Then Moses slew the ram, took of the blood, "and put it upon the tip of Aaron's right ear, and upon the thumb of his right hand, and upon the great toe of his right foot" (Ex. 29:20; Lev. 8:23). He put blood upon the same three points of Aaron's sons.

We understand that these three points represented their hearing, service, and walk of life. There is a children's song which says, "Be careful little ears what you hear, ... Be careful little hands what you do, ... Be careful little feet where you go." But why daub only the tip of one ear? No one hears with the tip of his ear! The tip is the very extremity of an ear, farthest from the inner ear. It is the last point that could possibly symbolize the hearing.

May we not thereby understand that God is concerned about the smallest portion of what we hear? He cares about peripheral misdeeds that only happen now and then, and those questionable places where we attend only once in awhile? The tip, the thumb, the toe—each represents an entire faculty: and true commitment includes the peripheral details as well as main-line activities. So beware of "*little* foxes, that spoil the vines" (Song of Sol. 2:15).

Moses "sprinkled the blood upon the altar round about" (Lev. 8:24b). Then he took the seven parts of the Consecration Ram, which God had specified to be burned for a sweet savour, together with unleavened bread, an unleavened cake tempered with oil, and an unleavened wafer anointed with oil (Ex. 29:2, 22-25; Lev. 8:25-28). All these he placed upon the hands of Aaron and his sons, waved them before the Lord, then burned all those pieces, and the bread, the cakes, and the wafer on the altar as a sweet savour unto the Lord.

Bread *unleavened* denotes freedom from sin, especially the absolute sinlessness of Christ Incarnate. Unleavened wafers *tempered* with oil speak of Jesus being filled with the Holy Spirit even before birth. Unleavened wafers *anointed* with oil typify His special anointing by the Holy Spirit, with power to fulfill in minute detail every part of His work.

Finally "Moses took of the anointing oil, and of the blood which was upon the altar, and sprinkled it upon Aaron, and upon his garments, and upon his sons, and upon his sons' garments with him; and sanctified Aaron, and his garments, and his sons, and his sons' garments with him" (Lev. 8:30).

Aaron and his sons boiled the remaining flesh of the Consecration Ram and ate it, with bread from the basket, at the door of the tabernacle. "And that which remaineth of the flesh and of the bread shall ye burn with fire" (Lev. 8:31, 32).

Thus the ceremonies of the first day were completed, but all these ceremonies needed to be repeated daily for seven days. "And thus shalt thou do unto Aaron, and to his sons,. . . seven days shalt thou consecrate them. . . ." (Ex. 29:35-37).

"And ye shall not go out of the door of the tabernacle of

the congregation in seven days, until the days of your consecration be at an end: for seven days shall he consecrate you.
. . . Therefore shall ye abide at the door of the tabernacle of
the congregation day and night seven days, . . . that ye die
not" (Lev. 8:33-35).

Abiding in the tabernacle for seven full days suggests the
imperative for Christians to abide in Christ ALWAYS, that
WE die not!

On the eighth day Aaron performed his first high priestly
duties, offering seven different sacrifices "and a meat offering mingled with oil" (Lev. 9:1-4). But why was he told to
offer a calf for his sin offering (9:1)? The sin offering for a
priest was to be a bullock (4:3). This calf may have been a
bullock, but Moses called it a calf. Was it to remind Aaron
of his principal sin, the golden calf that he had made (Ex.
32:1-6)? Surely that sin had to be properly atoned for before
Aaron could offer official sacrifices for others! First he
offered his own sin offering, then a ram for his burnt offering (9:7-14), after which he offered for others.

Because Jesus Christ was absolutely sinless, He needed no
sin offering for Himself like all other priests did. "For such
an high priest became us, who is holy, harmless, undefiled,
separate from sinners, and made higher than the heavens; who
needeth not daily, as those high priests, to offer up sacrifice,
first for his own sins, and then for the people's: for this he
did once, when he offered up himself. For the law maketh
men high priests which have infirmity; but the word of the
oath, which was since the law, maketh the Son, who is consecrated for evermore" (Heb. 7:26-28).

"But this man, after he had offered one sacrifice for sins
for ever, sat down on the right hand of God: from henceforth
expecting till his enemies be made his footstool. For by one
offering he hath perfected for ever them that are sanctified"
(Heb. 10:12-14).

Having been formed by God (Ps. 139:13-16), purchased,
cleansed, and redeemed by the blood of Christ, and endowed
with the Holy Spirit, we cannot afford to withhold from Him

any part of our person, possession, purpose or plans. *All are His!*

QUESTIONS FOR DISCUSSION

1. What does the initial washing of Aaron and his sons typify?
2. Why did Moses himself need to do all that washing?
3. With ankle-length coats, why were the breeches so important?
4. Why couldn't the priests put the Holy Garments on themselves?
5. How was the Tabernacle and all its vessels sanctified?
6. What did Moses do to the altar in addition to its anointing?
7. On how many heads did Moses "pour" the anointing oil?
8. What is meant by laying hands on the head of a sacrifice?
9. Why was the animal then immediately slain?
10. Which offerings were, and which were not, a sweet savor?
11. Of which could they eat, and of which could they not eat?
12. Which was all burnt on the altar? Which without the camp?
13. Name the several ways the Consecration Ram was utilized.
14. What all was done with the blood of the Consecration Ram?
15. What did Moses sprinkle on the priests and their garments?
16. What did they do with all the things in the basket?
17. How many animals did Moses slay in those seven days?
18. Where did Aaron and his sons stay those seven days and nights?

CHAPTER TEN

THE INCENSE ALTAR AND THE ANOINTING OIL

I. THE GOLDEN INCENSE ALTAR

Exodus 30:1-10; 37:25-28

"And thou shalt make an altar to burn incense upon: of shittim wood shalt thou make it. A cubit shall be the length thereof and a cubit shall be the breadth thereof; foursquare shall it be: and two cubits shall be the height thereof: the horns thereof shall be of the same. And thou shalt overlay it with pure gold, the top thereof, and the sides thereof round about, and the horns thereof; and thou shalt make unto it a crown of gold round about" (Ex. 30:1-10).

God instructed Moses about consecrating the priests (Ex. 29) before He introduced the Golden Altar. Perhaps one reason for this is because the Golden Altar represents Christ in His mediatorial role. "For there is one God, and one mediator between God and men, the *Man* Christ Jesus" (1 Tim.

2:5). Aaron and the Brazen Altar typified Christ in His sacri-
ficial role at Calvary. The Golden Altar stood squarely in front
of the Mercy Seat, depicting Christ interceding at God's right
hand for believers *today*.

Wood continues to typify Christ's humanity, for He is still
the MAN Christ Jesus. Gold continues to illustrate in typology what the Bible declares with authority: that in His very
essence and nature Jesus is also God. Isaiah, by inspiration
of the Holy Spirit, said He shall be called "The mighty God"
(9:6), using the same Hebrew word that is also translated "the
most high God" (Gen. 14:18, 19, 20, 22). "For in him
dwelleth all the fulness of the Godhead bodily" (Col. 2:9).

The horizontal dimensions, one cubit long and broad,
suggest the need for *unity* in human relationships. Two cubits
high, points to union and fellowship with Christ. This illustrates in type what both the Word and personal experience
plainly teach. If we neglect our horizontal relationships, it
mars our vertical fellowship. Husbands are admonished to
give honor unto their wives "as being heirs together of the
grace of life; that your prayers be not hindered" (1 Pet. 3:7).
To live selfishly, or to be inconsiderate of a wife's needs,
would certainly hinder our prayers.

While husband-and-wife relationships are of primary
importance, that is only part of the story. "Thou shalt not
defraud thy neighbor" (Lev. 19:13). "Devise not evil against
thy neighbor" (Prov. 3:29). "Honour thy father and thy
mother: and, thou shalt love thy neighbor as thyself" (Mt.
19:19). These are only a few of the many admonitions on
personal relationships; and that last clause is found eight
times in the New Testament. Many prayers are unheard and
fruitless because of faulty human relationships.

The Horns and the Crown (Ex. 30:2, 3)

Horns symbolize power (2 Chron. 18:10; Hab. 3:4). On the
Brazen Altar they emphasize the power of the Blood; on the
Golden Altar they signify the power of prayer. One horn on
each corner suggests that this power is equally available to

all people, and equally effective in all parts of the world.

The horns do not magnify the incense, which represents our prayers, but the Altar, which represents our Advocate with the Father, Jesus Christ the Righteous (1 John 2:1). Only in Him can we have power in prayer. Were it not for Him, our prayers would never reach heaven!

Praying *in Jesus' name* gives recognition to His preeminence and authority. There must be a conscious and diligent effort to pray according to His will, under His authority, and to His glory. To attach Jesus' name to a self-centered and selfish prayer is forgery, which God will not honor. We must remember that Jesus is our Legal Advocate as well as our Saviour. Because He is our Supreme Head in everything we do, we can neither worship effectively nor do business properly except in His name.

The Golden Crown is the shadow of Divine Royalty backing this Altar. The Brazen Altar, where the fires burned unendingly, has no crown. It represents Calvary where our Saviour suffered, bled, and died. Its brass speaks of judgment, and its horns denote the power of the blood. But the Crown on the Golden Altar declares the Victim of Calvary to now be the Victor over Satan, sin, and sorrow. He is "KING of Kings and LORD of lords," the Daysman (Job 9:33) who could lay His hands upon both God and man and reconcile wretched man unto a just and holy God! Through Him, and HIM ALONE, our prayers reach the throne of grace.

The Golden Altar stood just outside the Veil, squarely in front of the Mercy Seat (Ex. 30:6). Now Jesus has opened for us "a new and living way" (Heb. 10:20), through none other than Jesus Himself. The Veil is gone, and we may enter. "Let us therefore come boldly [BUT HUMBLY!] unto the throne of grace, that we may obtain mercy, and find grace to help in time of need" (Heb. 4:16).

Jesus' intercessory ministry makes Him the ultimate fulfillment of all that the Levitical priesthood stood for. We cannot bypass Calvary (self must still be crucified), nor the "washing of water by the word" (the Laver), nor forego the Living Bread at the Table of Fellowship. These are all vital parts of the process. But if it were not for Christ's intercessory ministry, we'd still be lost! Only once He died on Calvary, but ever since, He continues day and night as our Advocate (1 John 2:2), "seeing he ever liveth to make intercession for [us]" (Heb. 7:25).

Relationships are two-way affairs. Jesus most lovingly intercedes for us. We worship Him (and the Father through Him) in loving devotion expressed in adoration, praise, and thanksgiving as well as prayers, supplications, and intercessions. "Let my prayer be set forth before thee as incense; and the lifting up of my hands as the evening sacrifice" (Ps. 141:2).

The Golden Altar was intended for *sweet* incense (Ex. 30:7). Prayers should be well seasoned with love and devotion, lest we offer "strange incense" (v.9). "If I regard iniquity in my heart, the Lord will not hear me" (Ps. 66:18). Grudge, spite, and ill will are sins that clamp a lid on prayer. To clear the circuits for prayer, such attitudes must be unloaded at Calvary through Christ, God's Sin Offering and Burnt Sacrifice. Whatever has not been to Calvary is labeled "strange fire," a fatal risk if offered at the Golden Altar. Two sons of Aaron tried it and were burned to death by "fire from the Lord" (Lev. 10:1-3).

Aaron was to burn sweet incense upon this Altar every morning and every evening (Ex. 30:7,8). Once a day was not enough! Incense symbolizes the prayers of the saints (Rev. 8:3-5), and "prayer is the Christian's vital breath." Our bodies cannot survive without breathing and our spirits cannot thrive without prayer.

II. THE ANOINTING OIL

Exodus 30:22-33; 40:9-11; Leviticus 8:10-12, 30

Oil is considered symbolic of the Holy Spirit. Therefore it is understandable that all these vessels, and the Tabernacle itself, should be anointed with oil. Everyone of them represented certain aspects of our Lord Jesus Christ, our ultimate Example of Spirit anointing.

"And the spirit of the Lord shall rest upon him, the spirit of wisdom and understanding, the spirit of counsel and might, the spirit of knowledge and of the fear of the Lord" (Isa.11:2).

This arrangement may have been patterned after the Golden Lampstand. The "spirit of the LORD [Jehovah]," the central and principal one of the seven, corresponds well with the central stem upon which all the branches depend totally. The other six are named in pairs, like the three pairs of branches on the Lampstand. See the accompanying illustration.

The Anointing Oil was composed of four principal spices (Ex.30:23,24):

> 500 shekels of pure myrrh,
> 250 shekels of sweet cinnamon,
> 250 shekels of sweet calamus,
> 500 shekels of cassia.

Soltau[8] suggests that since *wisdom* and *understanding* are inseparable, pure myrrh may answer for the top pair of branches. [They are right in the center—in the very heart of it all.] And since *counsel* and *might* are totally different attributes,perhaps the cinnamon and calamus apply to the middle pair (each being only 250 shekels). Furthermore, since "all true *knowledge* is embodied in the *'fear of the Lord,'* "[8] the cassia may represent the third pair of branches. That would make five hundred shekels for each pair.

Be that as it may, we do know that this was "an oil of holy ointment, . . . an holy anointing oil" (Ex. 30:25). Of the Tabernacle and all its vessels God said, "Thou shalt anoint . . . and thou shalt sanctify them, that they may be most holy: whatsoever toucheth them shall be holy" (vv.26-29). These items in themselves were only metal, wood, and fiber; but set apart and sanctified to represent Jesus Christ, they are indeed holy.

This holy oil was poured upon Aaron's head also (Lev. 8:12) and was sprinkled (with blood of the Ram) upon all the priests and their garments to sanctify them (Lev. 8:30). All this points to the work of the Holy Spirit, even as the Golden Altar of Incense represents the mediatorial ministry of Christ today. Both are indispensable imperatives without which we would all be doomed!

This "oil of holy ointment" was strictly reserved for holy use. "Upon man's flesh shall it not be poured, neither shall ye make any other like it, . . . and it shall be holy unto you. Whosoever compoundeth any like it, or whosoever putteth any of it upon a stranger, shall even be cut off from his people" (Ex. 30:25, 32, 33). Also the perfume of sweet spices was not permitted for common use. "Whosoever shall make like unto it, to smell thereto, shall even be cut off from his people" (vv.34-38). What God sets apart for sacred purposes is holy, sanctified, and inviolable. "Be not deceived: God is not mocked."

QUESTIONS FOR DISCUSSION

1. Why, as Mediator, is Jesus called the MAN Christ Jesus?
2. What need was there for an Altar, just to offer incense?
3. Why were wood and gold both important for this Altar?
4. What was the significance in the specified dimensions?
5. What is the purpose of horns on an incense altar?
6. What, really, is the secret of power in prayer?
7. What is meant by "strange incense" and "strange fire"?

8. What does it mean to pray "in Jesus' name"?
9. What does the Crown of Gold on this Altar signify?
10. Why was there no crown on the Brazen Altar?
11. Was the precise location of the Golden Altar important?
12. Is there anything between the Mediator and Mercy Seat today?
13. Where and how did Jesus open a new and living way?
14. What does incense represent, and how often was it offered?
15. Where was the anointing oil used, and what did it symbolize?
16. Where was it NOT to be used, and why not?
17. What all did Moses sprinkle with blood and anointing oil?
18. Did that oil make the Tabernacle and all its vessels holy?

Dear Reader:
We have studied the furniture and the features of the Tabernacle. I trust you have studied it not only from this book, but straight from the Bible, as is suggested in the forepart of the book. It is my sincere prayer that it may have whetted your appetite for more and deeper Bible study, looking for Christ on every page of the Scriptures.

Jesus Christ is the key figure from Genesis through The Revelation, "For it pleased the Father that in him [in Christ Jesus] should all fulness dwell; . . . For in him dwelleth all the fulness of the Godhead bodily" (Col. 1:19; 2:9).

"The same was in the beginning with God. All things were made by him; and without him was not any thing made that was made . . . . He was in the world, and the world was made by him, and the world knew him not. He came unto his own, and his own received him not. But as many as received him, to them gave he power to become the sons of God, even to them that believe on his name" (John 1:2, 3, 10-12).

"Wherefore God also hath highly exalted him, and given him a name which is above every name: that at the name of Jesus every knee should bow, of things in heaven, and things in earth, and things under the earth; and that every tongue should confess that Jesus Christ is Lord, to the glory of God the Father" (Phil. 2:9-11). Let us confess him NOW. Waiting until Judgment Day is forever too late!

CHAPTER ELEVEN

THE PASSOVER AND THE DAY OF ATONEMENT

I. THE ANNUAL JEWISH PASSOVER

Exodus 12:1-51

The annual Passover was both memorial and symbolic: memorial in memory of that first passover night in Egypt; symbolic because its ultimate fulfillment was Calvary, "the Lamb of God, which taketh away the sin of the world" (John 1:29; 1 Cor. 5:7).

At the first Passover God revised the Hebrew calendar, making the first half of the Jewish Civil Year to be the last half of their Sacred Year. Abib, which was the seventh month, He said, "shall be unto you the beginning of months: it shall be the first month of the year to you" (Ex. 12:2). It was the month in which God brought the Israelites out of Egypt (Ex. 13:4; 23:15; 34:18; Dt. 16:1). To this day the Jews use both calendars. Their legal documents (like contracts, deeds, and births) are dated by the Civil Calendar, but all religious events (like their feast days) are dated by the Sacred Calendar.

During the Babylonian Captivity the name Abib was

changed to Nisan, found twice in the Bible (Neh. 2:1; Esther 3:7), and is still in use today. Nisan corresponds to the latter part of March and the forepart of April. The Jewish New Year, Rosh Hashanah, is still the first day of Tishri. Tishri corresponds to the latter part of September and the forepart of October.

A. The Observation Period.

On the tenth day of Abib (now Nisan), each family was to select a lamb, without blemish, a male of the first year, and keep it, apparently isolated and under close observation, until the fourteenth day (Ex. 12:3-6a). If it would have been injured or become sick during those four days, it would have been blemished. A replacement would have been necessary.

That four-day interval apparently prefigured the critical observation of Jesus the last four days before His crucifixion. On Palm Sunday He rode into Jerusalem on "a colt the foal of an ass . . . . And the multitudes that went before, and that followed, cried, saying, Hosanna to the Son of David: Blessed is he that cometh in the name of the Lord; Hosanna in the highest" (Mt. 21:5-9; Mark 11:8-10). This fulfilled Zechariah 9:9, and apparently identified Jesus as the Messiah, the real Antitype of the Passover lamb?

Jesus went into Jerusalem and cleansed the temple. "And when the chief priests and scribes saw the wonderful things that he did, and the children crying in the temple, and saying, Hosanna to the Son of David; they were sore displeased" (Mt. 21: 12-15). Mark, however, places the temple cleansing on Monday, after the cursing of the fig tree (Mk. 11:12-28).

Either way, a careful study of events reveals that Jesus was kept under critical scrutiny for four days. He was challenged by four different groups in one day: the chief priests and elders (Mt. 21:23-22:14); the Pharisees with the Herodians (vv.15-21); the Sadducees (vv.23-33); and the Pharisees with their lawyer (vv.34-46). It was a critical proving period, but every test proved Jesus to be the real Messiah, without spot or blemish.

Our calendars and manmade books practically all say Jesus

was crucified on Friday. It is true that "it was the preparation, that is, the day before the sabbath" (Mark 15:42), "and
the sabbath drew on" (Luke 23:54). But was not that a *special
sabbath*, of greater importance than the weekly sabbath? "The
next day was to be a *special Sabbath*" (John 19:31, NIV).[9]
"For that sabbath was an high day" (KJV).

The first day following Passover was indeed "an holy
convocation: ye shall do no servile work therein" (Lev. 23:5-
7; Ex. 12:15-17). It mattered not what day of the week it was.
"A special Sabbath" could well be on a Friday.

Various Harmonies of the Gospels list thirteen events
happening on Tuesday and eight on Thursday, leaving
Wednesday totally blank (apparently to delay the crucifixion
until Friday). Yet they list Tuesday as the day when Jesus said,
"Ye know that after two days is the feast of the passover, and
the Son of man is betrayed to be crucified" (Mt. 26:2). Would
not two days after Tuesday be Thursday? Are not the words
of Jesus more reliable than our calendars or manmade books?

Jesus declared that "as Jonah was three days and three
nights in the whale's belly; so shall the Son of man be three
days and three nights in the heart of the earth" (Mt. 12:40).
The four Gospel writers all present Him as being already risen
early Sunday morning, the first day of the week. But there
are only two nights between Friday evening and Sunday
morning!

B. The Lamb and the Blood

These are the symbols that matter more than which day or
what time of day Jesus was crucified! Yet God did specify
that the lamb was to be killed "in the evening," that is, in the
day's fourth quarter, between 3:00 and 6:00 P.M. by our reck-
oning of time. It was shortly after the ninth hour Hebrew time
(3:00 P.M. our time) when Jesus said, "Father, into thy hands
I commend my spirit: and having said thus, he gave up the
ghost" (Luke 23:44-46). Knowing all that, it was not by acci-
dent that God specified what time of day the Passover lamb
should die.

"And they shall take of the blood and strike it on the two

sideposts and on the upper door post [lintel] of the houses, wherein they shall eat it" (Ex. 12:7). For the blood to be shed and displayed in a vessel was not enough; it had to be applied. "And when I see the blood [applied] I will pass over you" (v.12). The Blood of Christ, shed for all men, avails nothing except for believers who appropriate its cleansing power by faith.

"And they shall eat the flesh in that night, roast with fire, . . . Eat not of it raw, nor sodden at all with water, but roast with fire; his head with his legs, and with the purtenance thereof. And ye shall let nothing of it remain until the morning; and that which remaineth of it until the morning ye shall burn with fire" (Ex. 12:8-10).

The lamb of course typified Christ, and with the cookware of that day the flesh could not be cooked without adding water. Christ shall not be *watered down*, nothing added to Him, and nothing taken away. The head, legs, and purtenance were not to be eaten, but the lamb was to be roasted whole, emphasizing that Christ is to be appropriated in His entirety: nothing added nor removed. The roasting denotes His suffering.

All that was not eaten was to be burned before morning. Typifying Christ, the lamb was holy. "Give not that which is holy unto the dogs" (Mt. 7:6). "Neither wilt thou suffer thine Holy One to see corruption" (Ps.16:10b). Those verses tell us why everything that was not eaten should be burned. Nothing should be left for the dogs, nor permitted to decay. The body of Christ saw no corruption in the grave.

II. THE FEAST OF UNLEAVENED BREAD

Exodus 12:15-20; Leviticus 23:4-8

Hebrew days begin in the evening, reckoned from sundown to sundown. Although the fourteenth day was to be leaven-free, the Feast of Unleavened Bread officially began with the beginning of the fifteenth day (Lev. 23:6). The reason is quite obvious. It symbolized deliverance and freedom from sin, which was obtained only through the offering of the Passover Lamb. "Without shedding of blood is no remission" (Heb. 9:22b). Deliverance and freedom was not obtained until the Lamb was offered and the blood applied. The fact that the Feast lasted seven days suggests that henceforth in Christ we should live in perpetual deliverance.

The Sheaf of the Firstfruits, typifying the Resurrection, was waved on the morrow after the [weekly] sabbath (Lev.23:9-14).

III. THE GREAT DAY OF ATONEMENT

Leviticus 16:1-34; 23:26-32

This was the sixth, and by far the most solemn, of the seven annual festivals that the Lord prescribed for Israel. The date for each was specified with divine purpose, and they are listed in chronological order (Lev. 23:4-32), by which an approximate time of the event typified may be perceived.

The Passover was first (Lev. 23:4, 5); then the seven-day Feast of Unleavened Bread (vv.6-8); during which the Sheaf of the First Fruits was waved on Easter Sunday, Resurrection morning (vv.9-14). That makes three events prefigured in twelve days. The Feast of Weeks (Pentecost) came seven weeks later (vv.15-21). The prophetic aspects of these four have been fulfilled.

The last three feasts came in the seventh month (Tishri), of which we await the full and final revelation in due time. The first day of the seventh month (Rosh Hashanah, the Jewish New Year) was the Blowing of Trumpets (Lev. 23:23-25); the tenth day was the Day of Atonement (vv.26-32); followed by the Feast of Tabernacles (vv.33-43), on the 15th through the 21st day).

The **DAY OF ATONEMENT** (tenth day of the seventh month) was the only day of the year in which the high priest (and he alone) could enter the Holy of Holies, "not without blood, which he offered for himself, and for the errors of the people" (Heb.9:7). He wore none of his colorful garments to enter behind the Veil. The people were to afflict their souls (Lev. 16:29-31; 23:32), foreshadowing a day of intense mourning (Zech. 12:9-14).

A. The Bullock: a Sin Offering for the High Priest
(Lev. 16:3, 4, 6, 11-14)

The high priest had to wash his flesh with water, put on the linen breeches, linen coat and girdle, and the linen mitre (Lev. 16:4). Then he first offered a bullock as a sin offering to make an atonement for himself and his house (vv.6, 11).

"And he shall take a censer full of burning coals of fire from off the altar before the Lord, and his hands full of sweet incense beaten small, and bring it within the veil and he shall put the incense upon the fire before the Lord, that the cloud of the incense may cover the mercy seat that is upon the testimony, that he die not: and he shall take of the blood of the bullock, and sprinkle it with his finger upon the mercy seat eastward; and before the mercy seat shall he sprinkle of the blood with his finger seven times" (16:12-14).

The high priest proceeded with utmost caution, "that he die not." Only after making this atonement for himself could the high priest offer a sin offering for the people.

B. The Goat: a Sin Offering for the People
(Lev. 16:5, 7, 15-16)

Then the high priest killed the goat that had been selected by lot (16:7, 8) to be the sin offering for the people. He brought of the goat's blood and sprinkled it seven times upon the mercy seat and seven times on the ground in front of the mercy seat, the same as he had done with the blood of the bullock.

Study verses 16-19 very carefully! Notice that the Tabernacle on both sides of the veil and all the vessels were sprinkled with the blood of the bullock and of the goat, even as Moses had "sprinkled all the vessels of the ministry" (Heb. 9:21). Notice also that he *"put* it upon the horns of the altar," that is, daubed it with his fingers.

Observe especially that not one person was permitted to

be with the high priest even in the forepart of the Sanctuary, from the beginning of this service until it was all finished (Lev. 16:17). Although "his own received him not" (John 1:11), Jesus Christ is the ONE AND ONLY High Priest   who can ever reconcile Israel (or anyone else) to God. This service focuses on the iniquities, transgressions, sins, and unclean-ness of Israel.

C. The Scapegoat

(Lev. 16:20-22)

Next the high priest brought the live goat, selected by lot (Lev.16:7, 8) to be the scapegoat. God, not man, decided which would die and which would be the sin-bearer. Jesus filled both roles. First He died to make an atonement for us. Then, "As far as the east is from the west, so far hath he removed our transgressions from us" (Ps. 103:12). Since the offered goat was not to be resurrected, it took a second goat to typify the sin-bearing aspects of Jesus' ministry to us.

"And Aaron shall lay both his hands upon the head of the live goat, and confess over him all the iniquities of the chil-dren of Israel, and all their transgressions in all their sins, putting them upon the head of the goat, and shall send him away by the hand of a fit man into the wilderness: and the goat shall bear upon him all their iniquities unto a land not inhabited: and he shall let go the goat in the wilderness" (16:21, 22).

There are various stories about what became of that goat, but since the Bible is silent about it, we will simply leave that with the Lord. The important message is that we must rely on Jesus to deliver us from sin and to remove our sins from us.

Some cultists teach that God puts our sins upon Satan, making Him our sin-bearer. Satan promotes all kinds of sin, and he can pile them on, but he can never remove one sin from anyone. Only Jesus Christ is able to do that! He is both able and willing even to "bear the iniquity of our holy things." Him will God honor as our Atonement and our continuing Advocate.

For these unique services thus far, the high priest wore only the linen garments, but now we see a change.

D. Further Activities

(Lev. 16:23-28)

For the rest of the Day's activities the high priest put off his linen garments, again washed his flesh with water, and put on his high priestly garments of gold, blue, purple, scarlet, and fine linen, for further duties. He offered burnt offerings, first for himself then for the people (v.24). He burnt the fat of the sin offerings upon the altar (v.25). He saw to it that the proper persons carried forth the bullock and the goat of the sin offerings, and completely burned them outside the camp. Compare Hebrews 13:11-13.

The fit man who had released the scapegoat and the one who burned the bullock and goat outside the camp, needed to wash their clothes and bathe their flesh, "and afterward come into the camp" (Lev. 16:26-28).

The animals offered on this day are not all named in this chapter. Moses Maimonides,[10] a Jewish rabbi, said there were fifteen in all. The two lambs for the continual burnt offering (Ex. 29:38-42) are not mentioned at all. Two rams for a burnt offering are mentioned briefly (Lev. 16:3, 5, 24). The bullock for Aaron's sin offering (vv.3, 6, 11-14, 18, 27), the goat for the congregation's sin offering (vv.5, 7-10, 15-19, 27), and the scapegoat (vv.7-10, 20-22, 26) are prominently treated.

We do not understand everything that is intended by the multiple sacrifices and services prescribed for Israel, but we do understand that they portray various aspects of our Lord and Saviour Jesus Christ, and that they emphasize in part the costliness of our salvation.

Some day we hope to sit in His typology class, listening with rapt attention, awe, and wonder as He expounds to us the truths and the types contained in the written Word, which we have studied for years and have failed to understand. Until then we only know in part. We praise and adore Him as best we know how, but we yearn for the day when we can worship Him with perfect praise, unhindered by the limitations of the flesh!

QUESTIONS FOR DISCUSSION

1. How and why did God revise the Hebrew calendar?
2. Name three events in the first month of the Sacred Calendar.
3. Name three events in the first month of the Civil Calendar.
4. Why did Jesus choose a donkey colt to ride into Jerusalem?
5. Who did the masses proclaim Him to be? Was it authentic?
6. What did the Observation Period prove Jesus to be?
7. What are the scriptural evidences of a Friday crucifixion?
8. Why was the Passover lamb to be killed "in the evening"?
9. Did it really matter where they put the blood?
10. Why could not the Feast of Unleavened Bread begin earlier?
11. To whom did the Sheaf of Firstfruits apply (1 Cor. 15:20-23)?
12. Was it waved after the *special* or after the *weekly* sabbath?
13. Why was the Day of Atonement an extremely solemn affair?
14. What did the high priest wear to enter the Holy of Holies?
15. What was he to do upon entering, "that he die not"?
16. How often did he sprinkle the Mercy Seat that day?
17. Why were the sin offering carcasses burned outside the camp?
18. Why did Aaron lay both hands on the head of the scapegoat?
19. What did it take to be a "fit man" to lead that goat away?
20. What did all active participants need to do afterward?

CHAPTER TWELVE

AARON, ELEAZAR, AND THE LEVITES

I. AARON AND ELEAZAR

"Aaron and his sons" are the first partnership of priests recorded in the Bible. Melchizedek was "the priest of the most high God" (Gen. 14:18). Evidently there was no associate priest; therefore there was no high priest. Aaron's sons were priests by virtue of being sons of Aaron.

Aaron and his sons together typified the spiritual priesthood of all true believers in the New Testament, who are priests only by virtue of being in Christ, our true High Priest. "Ye also . . . are built up a spiritual house, an holy priesthood, to offer up spiritual sacrifices, acceptable to God by Jesus Christ" (1 Pet. 2:5). He "hath made us kings and priests unto God" (Rev. 1:6; 5:10).

Aaron the high priest, in offering sacrifices, typified Christ in the flesh offering the Ultimate Sacrifice, of which all other sacrifices were only a shadow. Then in his death Aaron typified Christ ascending into heaven.

When Aaron's time came to die, God told Moses to bring Aaron and Eleazar up into Mount Hor, where Aaron was to die. Numbers 20:23-28. "Moses stripped Aaron of his garments, and put them upon Eleazar his son; and Aaron died there in the top of the mount: and Moses and Eleazar came down from the mount." Aaron died and God concealed the record of his burial. Aaron's going up and not returning typifies the Ascension of Christ.

Eleazar, however, returned in Aaron's stead, wearing the high priestly garments. Eleazar (the returning high priest) thereby typifies Christ in His Second Coming, whose imminent return the Church awaits with fond anticipation.

In our Introduction we said that the Tabernacle, a portable and temporary structure, typifies Christ and His Church on earth. While Aaron was living, Eleazar was to be "chief over the chief of the Levites, and have the oversight of them, that keep the charge of the sanctuary" (Nu. 3:32). To him also pertained the oil for the light, the incense, the anointing oil, and the oversight of all the tabernacle (4:16). In all this Eleazar typified Christ as Head of the Church throughout the church age.

In short, Aaron typified the ministry of Christ on earth, and Eleazar typified His ministry in heaven throughout the church age, which will be climaxed by His Coming Again!

II. THE LEVITES TYPIFIED THE CHURCH

Although it was not clearly revealed in the Old Testament, the Church "from the beginning of the world hath been hid in God, . . . to the intent that NOW unto the principalities and powers in heavenly places might be known *by the church* the manifold wisdom of God" (Eph. 3:9, 10). Truly, the New was in the Old concealed, and the Old is in the New revealed.

Comparing Scripture with Scripture we see how beautifully the tribe of Levi typifies the Church. "For the Lord had spoken unto Moses, saying, Only thou shalt not number the tribe of Levi, neither take the sum of them among the children of Israel: but thou shalt appoint the Levites over the tabernacle" (Nu. 1:48-50; 2:33).

"And I, behold, I have taken the Levites from among the children of Israel instead of all the firstborn . . . therefore the

Levites shall be mine;. . . mine shall they be: I am the Lord" (Nu. 3:12, 13, 41, 45). Likewise we, whom Christ "hath purchased with his own blood" (Acts 20:28), are verily God's property, for we "are bought with a price" (1 Cor. 6:19, 20).

Their Sanctification

"Take the Levites from among the children of Israel, and cleanse them.. . . . Sprinkle water of purifying upon them, and let them shave all their flesh, and let them wash their clothes, and so make themselves clean" (Nu. 8:6, 7). This is an outward similitude of a Christian's inner cleansing, "the washing of regeneration and renewing of the Holy Ghost" (Titus 3:5).

"And Aaron shall offer the Levites before the Lord for an offering of the children of Israel, that they may execute the service of the Lord" (Nu. 8:11). "For they are wholly given unto me . . . even instead of the firstborn . . . have I taken them unto me" (8:16).

"And I have given the Levites as a gift to Aaron and to his sons . . ., to do the service of the children of Israel in the tabernacle of the congregation" (Nu. 8:19). Levi means "joined unto" (Gen. 29:34), and God said the Levites shall be "joined unto" Aaron (Nu. 18:2, 4), even as the church is joined unto Christ.

All this corresponds well with Christ and His Church. Aaron's priesthood did not equal, but certainly typified, the Priesthood of Christ. The setting apart and ceremonial cleansing of the Levites portrayed the inner cleansing and sanctification of the Church. The Levites were "wholly given" to God, who then gave them "as a gift to Aaron." That is almost identical with what Jesus said in His High Priestly prayer. "The men which thou gavest me out of the world: thine they were, and thou gavest them me;. . . I pray . . . for them which thou hast given me, for they are thine" (John 17:6, 9).

The Levites did not Go to War

Nonresistance, as prescribed in the New Testament for the

Church, was not required of national Israel. Moses requested the two and a half tribes who settled on the east side of Jordan, to "go armed before the Lord to war,. . . But if ye will not do so, behold, ye have sinned before the Lord: and be sure your sin will find you out" (Nu. 32:20-23). And God commanded King Saul to "go and smite Amalek, and utterly destroy all that they have, and spare them not; but slay both man and woman, infant and suckling, ox and sheep, camel and ass" (1 Sam. 15:3).

But from the day that the Levites were set apart, cleansed and sanctified similar to the Church, the LEVITES DID NOT GO TO WAR, not even for noncombatant service! There were no Levites among the twelve spies (Nu. 13:4-15). This, in a practical way, foreshadowed Biblical nonresistance for the Church.

Their Unique Inheritance

"Levi hath no part nor inheritance with his brethren; the Lord is his inheritance, according as the Lord thy God promised him" (Dt. 10:9). "And the Lord spake unto Aaron, Thou shalt have no inheritance in their land, neither shalt thou have any part among them: for I am thy part and thine inheritance among the children of Israel (Nu. 18:20).

Levi's noninheritance status typifies the stranger and pilgrim concept of the church on earth: not claiming political franchise, but functioning as "ambassadors for Christ" (2 Cor. 5:20). We represent Christ's interests on earth, but "our citizenship is in heaven" (Phil. 3:20, NKJ). [11]

"The tithes of the children of Israel, which they offer as an heave offering unto the Lord, I have given to the Levites to inherit: therefore I have said unto them, Among the children of Israel they shall have no inheritance" (Nu. 18:24).

To the Levites God said, "When ye take of the children of Israel the tithes which I have given you from them for your inheritance, then ye shall offer up an heave offering of it for the Lord, even a tenth part of the tithe" (Nu. 18:26). Then, even as now, everybody needed the benefit of tithing!

The Levitical Exemption

Israel had arrived at the southern end of the Promised Land, and twelve spies had searched the land. Ten of them had seen more of the giants than they remembered of God. Their evil report discouraged the people, igniting riotous murmuring among the people (Nu. 13:26-33). "Would God that we had died in the land of Egypt," they groaned; and, "Would God we had died in this wilderness" (14:2).

God took the murmurers at their word and said, "Your carcasses *shall* fall in this wilderness; and all that were numbered of you . . . from twenty years old and upward, which have murmured against me, doubtless ye shall not come into the land,. . . save Caleb ... and Joshua" (14:29, 30). That numbering included "every male from twenty years old and upward, all that were able to go forth to war." Those were the numbering stipulations spelled out in those words thirteen times in Numbers 1:20-45.

"But the Levites . . . were not numbered among them" (1:47), nor "among the children of Israel" (1:49; 2:33). They were not eligible to go forth to war, nor to be numbered from twenty years old and upward. The Levites were numbered from one month old and upward (3:15), with no claim to personal abilities.

So the death sentence as pronounced in Numbers 14:29, 30, did not include the Levites. They, with all the other tribes, wandered in the wilderness for another thirty-eight years, "until all the generation of the men of war were wasted out from among the host, as the Lord sware unto them" (Dt. 2:14, 16).

It is certainly true that "all the men of war, died in the wilderness" (Josh. 5:4); "till all the people that were men of war, . . . were consumed" (5:6). That did not include the Levites. They were numbered separately, and exempt from war.

Eleazar certainly was more than twenty years old when the children of Israel left Egypt, and we are not sure about his son Phinehas (Ex. 6:25). They both entered the Promised Land as prominent leaders, instead of dying in the wilderness.

SUMMARY

The Tabernacle and all its features, the priests and all their services, the multiple sacrifices with all their rituals, were only a foreshadow of the coming ministry of Jesus Christ! The Levites with all their favored blessings were only a shadow of what the Church enjoys in Christ today. And our blessings today are only "the earnest [preliminary evidence] of our inheritance until the redemption of the purchased possession, unto the praise of [Christ's] glory" (Eph. 1:14). "In the ages to come he [will] shew the EXCEEDING RICHES OF HIS GRACE" (2:7)!

QUESTIONS FOR DISCUSSION

1. What did Aaron and his sons together typify?
2. What aspects of Christ's First Advent were typified in Aaron?
3. Why do you think Aaron's burial was kept out of the record?
4. What of Christ's present ministry was typified in Eleazar?
5. Why were the Levites not numbered with the other tribes?
6. By what act had they shown distinguished loyalty to God?
7. How and why were they numbered differently from the others?
8. What capability was essential in numbering the other tribes?
9. In what ways were the Levites like the Christian church?
10. What all did they inherit instead of land or possessions?
11. Why were they to give a tenth of the tithes they received?
12. Who benefits more from tithing, the giver or the receiver?
13. What is the basic difference between the two benefits?
14. Who is the "purchased possession" in Ephesians 1:14?
15. What is meant by the redemption of that possession?

LIST OF ABBREVIATIONS USED
IN THIS BOOK

Old Testament Books

Gen.	Genesis			
Ex.	Exodus			
Lev.	Leviticus			
Nu.	Numbers			
Dt.	Deuteronomy			
Josh.	Joshua			
Sam.	Samuel			
Chron.	Chronicles			
Neh.	Nehemiah			
Esth.	Esther			
Ps .	Psalm			
Prov.	Proverbs			
Eccl.	Ecclesiastes			
S. of Sol.	Song of Solomon			
Isa.	Isaiah			
Jer.	Jeremiah			
Ezek.	Ezekiel			
Dan.	Daniel			
Hos.	Hosea			
Obad.	Obadiah			
Hab.	Habakkuk			
Zeph.	Zephaniah			
Hag.	Haggai			
Zech.	Zechariah			
Mal.	Malachi			

New Testament Books

Mt.	Matthew
Mk.	Mark
Lu.	Luke
Rom.	Romans
Cor.	Corinthians
Gal.	Galatians
Eph.	Ephesians
Phil.	Phillipians
Col.	Colossians
Thess.	Thessalonians
Tim.	Timothy
Heb.	Hebrews
Pet.	Peter
Rev.	Revelation

FOOTNOTES

1. Glenn M.Jones, *Big Ten Tabernacle Topics*, Moody Press, Chicago, page 38.

2. God *built* a wife for Adam (Gen. 2:22, Hebrew and German) Christ's Church is built (Mt. 16:18), not created.

3. Longfellow, Henry W., *Psalm of Life.*

4. *JOSEPHUS, The Works of FLAVIUS, Antiquities of the Jews*, Book III, Chapter VI, page 72.

5. *JOSEPHUS*, ibidim

6. James 5:9b, *New King James Version*, copyright 1982 by permission from Thomas Nelson Inc., Nashville, TN

7. Soltau, Henry W., *The Tabernacle*, Kregel Publications, Grand Rapids, Michigan, page 354

8. Ibidim, page 348

9. John 19:31, *New International Version*, copyright 1978 by permission from International Bible Society, Colorado Springs, CO

10. Moses Maimonides, a Jewish rabbi, philosopher, and writer (1135-1204 A.D) was well acquainted with Jewish rituals. Years ago somewhere I picked up his statement about the fifteen animals, and wrote it down. But the source of that quote, except the author, is unknown to me. Maimonides is listed in our encyclopedias, but this quote I do not find.

11. Philippians 3:20a, *New King James Version*, by permission. op. cit.

BIBLIOGRAPHY

Buksbazen, Victor, *The Gospel in the Feasts of Israel* (Christian Literature Crusade, Fort Washington, PA, 1990).

Byler, Dan J.B., *The Shadow of the Cross* (Historic Christian Publishers., Seymour, Missouri.)

Habershon, Ada, *The Study of the Types,* and, *Outline Studies of the Tabernacle* (Kregel Publications, Grand Rapids, MI, 1974)

Hession, Roy, *From Shadow to Substance* (Christian Literature Crusade, Fort Washington, PA, 1977).

Ironside, H. A., *The Levitical Offerings* (Loizeaux Brothers, Neptune, NJ, 1982).

Jantzi, Leonard N., with manuscripts by C. K. Zehr (deceased), *The Way to a Holy God by the Tabernacle Study* (Edited and designed by Amish Publishing Service, Aylmer, Ont. Printed by Schlabach Printers, Sugarcreek, OH, 1980).

Jones, Glenn M., *Big Ten Tabernacle Topics* (Moody Press, Chicago, 1967).

Levy, David M., *The Tabernacle: Shadows of the Messiah* (The Friends of Israel Gospel Ministry, Inc., Bellmawr, NJ, 1993).

Master, John R., *Timely Truths from the Tabernacle* (Regular Baptist Press, Schaumburg, IL, 1981).

Pink, Arthur W., *Gleanings in Exodus* (Moody Press, Chicago, 1973).

Rockford, Perry F., *The Tabernacle* (The Peoples Gospel Hour, Halifax, Canada).

Stemming, C. W., *These Are the Garments* (Christian Literature Crusade, Fort Washington, PA, 1983).

Soltau, Henry W., *The Tabernacle* (Kregel Publications, Chicago, IL).

Tasker, R.V.G., *The Old Testament in the New Testament* (Wm. B. Eerdmans Publishing Co., Grand Rapids, MI, 1968).

Wilson, Walter Lewis, *Wilson's Dictionary of Bible Types* (Wm. B. Eerdmans Publishing Co. Grand Rapids, MI, 1957).

Zehr, Paul M., *God Dwells With His People* (Herald Press, Scottdale, PA; Kitchener, Ont., 1981).

JESUS CHRIST:

THE ONE AND ONLY WAY TO HEAVEN

Jesus pleads invitingly, "I am the **way**, the **truth**, and the **life**: no man cometh to the Father, but by me" (John 14:6). "Verily, verily, . . . I am the door of the sheep" (10:7).

"Neither is there salvation in any other: for there is none other name under heaven given among men, whereby we must be saved" (Acts 4:12).

But to claim His name without the new life (2 Cor. 5:17), is a fatal deception! Jesus lovingly cautions, "Not every one that saith unto me, Lord, Lord, shall enter the kingdom of heaven; but he that **doeth** the will of my Father" (Mt. 7:21-23).

"I am the vine, ye are the branches: . . . If a man *abide not in me, he is cast forth as a branch*, and is withered; . . . and they are burned" (John 15:5, 6).

Romans eight, obviously written for Christians, list 34 blessings especially for Christians. It solemnly warns against empty profession, but offers glorious assurance for those who *abide in Christ, and bear fruit. "For if ye live after the flesh, **ye shall die:** but if ye through the Spirit do mortify the deeds of the body, **ye shall live"** (8:13).

Seven Secrets for Eternal Life in Christ. We must:
- confess our sins (1 John 1:9), and sinful nature (Isa. 64:6).
- crucify sin and self (Rom. 6:6-13; Gal. 2:20; Col. 3:3).
- be washed by **faith** in the blood of Christ (Eph. 5:26, 27).
- confess and receive Christ as **Savior** and **Lord** (Rom. 10:9, 10).
- be born not of flesh but of **God** (John 1:13; 1 Cor. 15:50), of water [the **word**] and the **Spirit** (John 3:3-5).
- **REPENT**, be baptized, and be filled with the Spirit (Acts 2:38).
- **BELIEVE, OBEY and FULLY TRUST IN CHRIST.**

"He that hath the Son hath life; and he that hath not the Son of God hath not life" (I John 5:12).

More From Ervin N. Hershberger

The late Ervin N. Hershberger condensed a lifetime of Old Testament study and teaching into three succinct books: *Seeing Christ in the Tabernacle, Seeing Christ in the Old Testament,* and *God at Work in Saints of Old.* Hershberger also penned a fourth book, *God's Wake-up Call* which is a wake-up call from the New Testament. If you enjoyed *Seeing Christ in the Tabernacle* you will want to make sure and get your hands on the other three books. You can order them by using the convenient order form in the back of this book.

Seeing Christ in the Old Testament

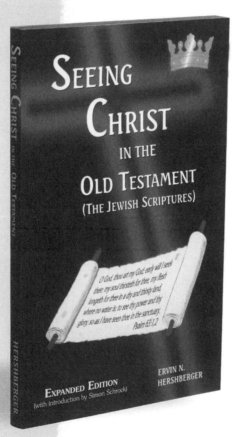

Hershberger finds 69 pictures of Christ in the first 31 verses of the Bible. He shows how Christ is the meaning and fulfillment of every Hebrew name for God. His account highlights surprising types and shadows of Christ in the lives of Adam, Noah, Joseph, David, Elijah, Elisha, and others. The appearances of God in the Old Testament are convincingly shown to be pictures of Christ. These pictures are affirmed in the words of Jesus: "In the volume of the book it is written of me."

To order, use the order form in the back of this book

God at Work in Saints of Old

"Lives of great men all remind us we can make our lives sublime, and departing, leave behind us footprints on the sands of time" (Longfellow). You can read the secret of such lives in this book. The 21 Bible characters it describes faced hard decisions just as you do. They were not aware that their actions would transform the ordinary into the extraordinary.

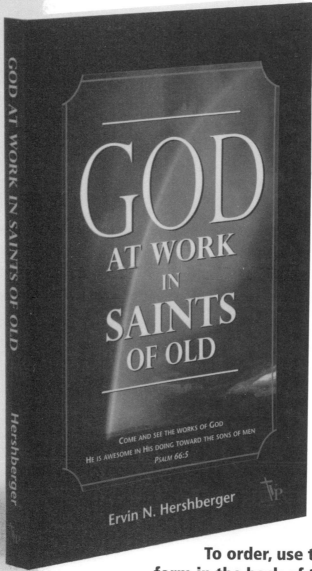

GOD AT WORK IN SAINTS OF OLD

Hershberger

GOD
AT WORK
IN
SAINTS
OF OLD

COME AND SEE THE WORKS OF GOD
HE IS AWESOME IN HIS DOING TOWARD THE SONS OF MEN
PSALM 66:5

Ervin N. Hershberger

To order, use the order form in the back of this book

God's Wake-up Call

A Wake-up Call From the New Testament

Ervin Hershberger's culminating work details nine urgent warnings for end times saints. Guard against covetousness and carelessness. Wake out of indifference and deafness to Christ. Be encouraged as you become more aware of God's marvelous provision for all your needs!

To order, use the order form in the back of this book

Order Form

To order, send this completed order form to:
Vision Publishers
P.O. Box 190
Harrisonburg, VA 22803
Fax 540-437-1969
E-mail: orders@vision-publishers.com
www.vision-publishers.com

_____   _____
Name   Date

_____   _____
Mailing Address   Phone

_____   _____
City   State   Zip

Seeing Christ in the Old Testament   Quantity_____ x $5.99 each = _____

Seeing Christ in the Tabernacle   Quantity_____ x $5.99 each = _____

God at Work in Saints of Old   Quantity_____ x $5.99 each = _____

God's Wake-up Call   Quantity_____ x $3.99 each = _____

Price _____

Virginia residents add 5% sales tax _____

Ohio residents add applicable sales tax _____

Shipping & handling __**$4.50**__

Grand Total _____

☐ Check #_____   **All payments in US Dollars**

☐ Money Order   ☐ Visa

☐ MasterCard   ☐ Discover

Name on Card _____

Card # __|__|__|__| __|__|__|__| __|__|__|__| __|__|__|__|

3-digit code from signature panel __|__|__| Exp. Date __|__|__|__|

Thank you for your order!

For a complete listing of our books write for our catalog.
Bookstore inquiries welcome.

Order Form

To order, send this completed order form to:
Vision Publishers
P.O. Box 190
Harrisonburg, VA 22803
Fax 540-437-1969
E-mail: orders@vision-publishers.com
www.vision-publishers.com

Name   Date

Mailing Address   Phone

City   State   Zip

Seeing Christ in the Old Testament   Quantity_____ x $5.99 each = _____

Seeing Christ in the Tabernacle   Quantity_____ x $5.99 each = _____

God at Work in Saints of Old   Quantity_____ x $5.99 each = _____

God's Wake-up Call   Quantity_____ x $3.99 each = _____

Price _____

Virginia residents add 5% sales tax

Ohio residents add applicable sales tax _____

Shipping & handling ___**$4.50**___

Grand Total _____

☐ Check #_____   **All payments in US Dollars**

☐ Money Order   ☐ Visa

☐ MasterCard   ☐ Discover

Name on Card _____

Card # __|__|__|__| __|__|__|__| __|__|__|__| __|__|__|__|

3-digit code from signature panel __|__|__| Exp. Date __|__|__|__|

Thank you for your order!

For a complete listing of our books write for our catalog.
Bookstore inquiries welcome.

List of Bookstores Handling Our Books

CALIFORNIA
Squaw Valley
Sequoia Christian Books
559/332-2606

COLORADO
Fruita
Grand Valley Dry Goods
970/858-1268

FLORIDA
Miami
Alpha and Omega
305/273-1263
Orlando
Borders Books and Music
407/826-8912

GEORGIA
Glennville
Vision Bookstore
912/654-4086
Montezuma
The Family Book Shop
478/472-5166

ILLINOIS
Arthur
Arthur Distributor Company
217/543-2166
Clearview Fabrics and Books
217/543-9091
Miller's Dry Goods
175-E County Road 50-N
Ava
Pineview Books
584 Bollman Road

INDIANA
Goshen
Miller's Country Store
574/642-3861
R And B's Kuntry Store
574/825-0191
Shady Walnut Grocery
574/862-2368

LaGrange
Pathway Bookstore
2580 North 250 West
Middlebury
F and L Country Store
574/825-7513
Laura's Fabrics
55140 County Road 43
Nappanee
Little Nook Bookstore
574/642-1347
Odon
Dutch Pantry
812/636-7922
Schrock's Kountry Korner
812/636-7842
Shipshewana
E and S Sales
260/768-4736
Wakarusa
Maranatha Christian Bookstore
574/862-4332

IOWA
Carson
Refining Fires Books
712/484-2214
Kalona
Friendship Bookstore
2357 540th Street SW

KANSAS
Hutchinson
Gospel Book Store
620/662-2875
Moundridge
Gospel Publishers
620/345-2532

KENTUCKY
Manchester
Lighthouse Ministries
606/599-0607

**Our books may also be found on many
Choice Books bookracks and Lantern Books bookracks**

Stephensport
Martin's Bookstore
270/547-4206

LOUISIANA
Belle Chasse
Good News Bookstore
504/394-3087

MARYLAND
Grantsville
Shady Grove Market and
  Fabrics
301/895-5660
Hagerstown
J. Millers Gospel Store
240/675-0383
Landover
Integrity Church Bookstore
301/322-3311
Oakland
Countryside Books and More
301/334-3318
Silver Spring
Potomac Adventist Bookstore
301/572-0700
Union Bridge
Hege's Catalog Store
410/775-7643

MICHIGAN
Burr Oak
Chupp's Herbs and Fabric
269/659-3950
Charlotte
Meadow Ridge Woodcrafts LLC
517/543-8680
Clare
Colonville Country Store
989/386-8686
Snover
Country View Store
989/635-3764

MISSOURI
Advance
Troyer's Grocery
573/722-3406

La Russell
Schrock's Kountry Korner
417/246-5351
Rutledge
Zimmerman's Store
660/883-5766
Seymour
Byler Supply & Country Store
417/935-4522
Shelbyville
Windmill Ridge Bulk Foods
4100 Highway T
Versailles
Excelsior Bookstore
573/378-1925
Weatherby
Country Variety Store
816/449-2932
Windsor
Rural Windsor Books and
  Variety
660/647-2705

NEW MEXICO
Farmington
Lamp and Light Publishers
505/632-3521

NEW YORK
Seneca Falls
Sauder's Store
315/568-2673

NORTH CAROLINA
Blanch
Yoder's Country Market
336/234-8072
Greensboro
Borders Books and Music
336/218-0662
Raleigh
Borders Books and Music #365
919/755-9424

NORTH DAKOTA
Mylo
Lighthouse Bookstore
701/656-3331

Our books may also be found on many
Choice Books bookracks and Lantern Books bookracks

OKLAHOMA
Miami
Eicher's Country Store
918/540-1871
OHIO
Berlin
Christian Aid Ministries
330/893-2428
Gospel Book Store
330/893-2523
Brinkhaven
Little Cottage Books
740/824-3808
Dalton
Little Country Store
330/828-8411
Fredricksburg
Faith-View Books
330/674-4129
Leetonia
Tinkling Spring Country Store
330/482-4592
Mesopotamia
Eli Miller's Leather Shop
440/693-4448
Middlefield
S & E Country Store
440/548-2347
Millersburg
Country Furniture & Bookstore
330/893-4455
Plain City
Deeper Life Bookstore
614/873-1199
Seaman
Keim Family Market
937/386-9995
Sugarcreek
JSR Fabric and Shoes
330/852-2721
The Gospel Shop
330/852-4223
Troyer's Bargain Store
2101 County Road 70

OREGON
Estacada
Bechtel Books
530/630-4606
Halsey
Shoppe of Shalom
541/369-2369
PENNSYLVANIA
Amberson
Scroll Publishing Co.
717/349-7033
Belleville
Yoder's Gospel Book Store
717/483-6697
Chambersburg
Burkholder Fabrics
717/369-3155
Pearson's Pasttimes
717/267-1415
Denver
Weaver's Store
717/445-6791
Ephrata
Clay Book Store
717/733-7253
Conestoga Bookstore
717/354-0475
Home Messenger Library &
Bookstore
717/351-0218
Ken's Educational Joys
717/351-8347
Gordonville
Ridgeview Bookstore
717/768-7484
Greencastle
Country Dry Goods
717/593-9661
Guys Mills
Christian Learning Resource
814/789-4769
Leola
Conestoga Valley Bookbindery
717/656-8824

Our books may also be found on many
Choice Books bookracks and Lantern Books bookracks

Lewisburg
Crossroads Gift and Bookstore
570/522-0536
McVeytown
Penn Valley Christian Retreat
717/899-5000
Meadville
Gingerich Books and Notions
814/425-2835
Monroe
Border's Books and Music
412/374-9772
Mount Joy
Mummau's Christian Bookstore
717/653-6112
Myerstown
Witmer's Clothing
717/866-6845
Newville
Corner Store
717/776-4336
Rocky View Bookstore
717/776-7987
Parkesburg
Brookside Bookstore
717/692-4759
Quarryville
Countryside Bargains
717/528-2360
Shippensburg
Mt. Rock Bookstore
717/530-5726
Springboro
Chupp's Country Cupboard
814/587-3678

SOUTH CAROLINA
Barnwell
The Genesis Store
803/541-6109
North Charleston
World Harvest Ministries
843/554-7960
Summerville
Manna Christian Bookstore
843/873-4221

Sumter
Anointed Word Christian
  Bookstore
803/494-9894
TENNESSEE
Crossville
MZL English Book Ministry
931/277-3686
Troyer's Country Cupboard
931/277-5886
Deer Lodge
Mt. Zion Literature Ministry
931/863-8183
Paris
Miller's Country Store
731/644-7535
Sparta
Valley View Country Store
931/738-5465
TEXAS
Kemp
Heritage Market and Bakery
903/498-3366
Seminole
Nancy's Country Store
432/758-9162
VIRGINIA
Bristow
The Lighthouse Books
703/530-9039
Dayton
Books of Merit
540/879-2628
Mole Hill Books & More
540/867-5928
Rocky Cedars Enterprises
540/879-9714
Harrisonburg
Christian Light Publications
540/434-0768
McDowell
Sugar Tree Country Store
540/396-3469

**Our books may also be found on many
Choice Books bookracks and Lantern Books bookracks**

Rural Retreat
Bender's Fabrics
276/686-4793
Woodbridge
Mennonite Maidens
703/622-3018
WASHINGTON
North Bonneville
Moore Foundation
800/891-5255
WEST VIRGINIA
Renick
Yoders' Select Books
304/497-3990
WISCONSIN
Dalton
Mishler's Country Store
West 5115 Barry Rd.
Granton
Mayflower Country Store
715/238-7988
South Wayne
Pilgrim's Pantry
608/439-1064

CANADA
BRITISH COLUMBIA
Burns Lake
Wildwood Bibles and Books
250/698-7451
Montney
Janice Martin Books
250/327-3231
MANITOBA
Arborg
Sunshine Christian Books
204/364-3135
ONTARIO
Aylmer
Mennomex
519/773-2002
Brunner
Country Cousins
519/595-4277
Lighthouse Books
519/595-4500
Floradale
Hillcrest Home Baking and Dry
Goods
519/669-1381
Linwood
Living Waters Christian
Bookstore
519/698-1198
Mount Forest
Shady Lawn Books
519/323-2830
Newton
Canadian Family Resources
519/595-7585

Our books may also be found on many
Choice Books bookracks and Lantern Books bookracks